The MAHA COOKBOOK

TAKING CHARGE OF YOUR HEALTH WITH VIBRANT, WHOLE FOODS

PETE EVANS

MAHA BOOKS

I dedicate this book to all the passionate, courageous, open-hearted, open-minded individuals and families who seek to find simple, nature-focused solutions for long-term regenerative health. Many say this way of life is extreme, whereas I view it as a beautiful adventure of self-love and nourishment that can be shared with others.

Cook, Eat, and Live with Love and Laughter.

—Cheers, Pete xo

A portion of the proceeds goes to MAHA Action 501(c)4.

MAHA Books books may be purchased in bulk at special discounts for sales promotion, corporate gifts, fund-raising, or educational purposes. Special editions can also be created to specifications. For details, contact the Special Sales Department, Skyhorse Publishing, 307 West 36th Street, 11th Floor, New York, NY 10018 or info@skyhorsepublishing.com.

MAHA Books is an imprint of Skyhorse Publishing, Inc.®, a Delaware corporation.

Visit our website at www.skyhorsepublishing.com.

Please follow our publisher Tony Lyons on Instagram @tonylyonsisuncertain.

10 9 8 7 6 5 4 3 2 1

Library of Congress Control Number: 2025944755

Cover design by Kai Texel
Cover and interior photographs courtesy of the author

Print ISBN: 978-1-964219-14-1
Ebook ISBN: 978-1-964219-15-8

Printed in the United States of America

Contents

PART I
Welcome to the MAHA Movement

INTRODUCTION

Fifteen years ago, I started on a wonderful journey of discovery that allowed me to understand, at a very deep and heartfelt level, that "food is medicine," and for that I am ever so very grateful. At the time, I was burdened with an extra twenty to thirty pounds of my own doing. I was bloated and inflamed and just feeling pretty flat most of the time. I thought, *There has to be another way to use my skills as a chef to turn my situation around, and to not only find solutions, but to put them into action.* Then I made a profound choice: I was going to learn about real nutrition and the power that real food can have, not only for myself but for the wider community. Real food, straight from the earth, cooked with LOVE.

Finding the secret recipe/s that could help me was the first hurdle, as there is so much information from organizations such as government-backed dietitians/dietetic associations around the world, the social media influencers, and everything in between. I understand it can be so overwhelming for anyone who wishes to simply find the answer as to what we should eat for long-term regenerative health. When you think about it, every other species on the planet, either instinctively or intuitively, knows what to eat. It shouldn't be rocket science to us (human beings that are considered one of the most intelligent species on the planet). Then why is this simple question of what should we eat so confusing with so many different viewpoints? And how is it that we can look at one study that allegedly proves one thing, and then find another that proves the exact opposite? Is this on purpose, or have we become so disconnected from our nature and from nature itself that what we might really need is that deeper connection to nature as the starting point?

This reconnection to nature is what I, and many others, believe is one of the fundamental and foundational pillars to MAHA. And just for a quick overview, the information I share in this book, including the recipes, have helped countless people from all over the world including myself not only improve their health but reclaim it in the most powerful ways. As I sit here writing this at the age of fifty-two years young, I am in the best physical and emotional state I have ever been in, which is what so many people have shared with me too, whether they are in their teens or their eighties. So, let's go on a journey together over the coming chapters that gives a greater insight into that very much needed invitation to foster a deeper respect, recognition, and relationship to nature

CHAPTER 1

What Is MAHA?

MAHA simply stands for Make America Healthy Again, and I love that it also stands for Make Australia Healthy Again, as I am an Australian who has spent many years working and traveling throughout the USA and have found that both countries have some deadly serious health issues going on . . . as do many countries in the Western world. So why is MAHA resonating deeply with people at the moment, and how has it become a movement unlike any we have witnessed before? Some even believe it contributed to a president being elected recently, and it was this MAHA movement that pushed the vote over the line. The simple answer is that people are not just wishing for but are demanding change on many different levels in regard to not only individual health, but all the way up to the top echelons of government institutions. MAHA includes, but is not limited to, the very important foundations that create our food supply and a whole lot more. This is what Robert (Bobby) Kennedy Jr. has pledged to investigate over the coming years, and he has sworn to be transparent with his and his team's findings.

Now, I've seen families from Sydney to Seattle transform, just by choosing better food. That's the heart of MAHA, which, in its most simple definition, is a movement to make health simple, joyful, and within reach for everyone.

I have been inspired by the MAHA Commission's groundbreaking report, released on May 22, 2025, in which MAHA challenges us (or, as I like to say, *invites* us) to exclude or reduce ultra-processed foods—those sugary, additive-laden culprits which seem to be behind so many chronic illnesses—and celebrate and embrace whole foods like grass-fed and finished beef, wild salmon, and pesticide-free vegetables and seasonal fruits. However, it's not about perfection or fancy diets. Whether you're a busy parent, a curious single, or a seasoned cook, MAHA can meet you where you are. It's one meal, one choice, one step toward feeling like yourself again. My thirty-plus cookbooks since my epiphany fifteen years ago have been about just that: making healthy eating accessible, delicious, and fun for individuals and families everywhere.

At the helm of this movement is my dear friend, Robert F. Kennedy Jr., whose leadership as Health and Human Services Secretary and chair of the MAHA Commission has lit a fire under us all. When Bobby and President Trump announced MAHA, I was thrilled—here was a vision that echoed my own, then backed by a report that pinpointed poor diet, environmental toxins, and overmedicalization as drivers of chronic disease. Bobby's resilience, pushing forward despite relentless criticism, inspires me. He's faced more pushback than most, yet he leads with love, rallying a community of moms sourcing farm-fresh eggs, dads grilling nutrient-packed dinners, doctors questioning outdated norms, and passionate folks from coast to coast. Together, they're building a healthier future, one kitchen at a time. Their stories remind me of the tens of thousands I've heard since launching my award-winning documentary many years ago, *The Magic Pill*, on how food can be medicine from people who found real health by choosing real food and eliminating others.

Of course, not everyone loves this message. Years before COVID, when I started sharing stories of people improving their health and reversing many chronic conditions and even reducing or getting off pharmaceuticals all together, some folks (the media, old school dietitians, medical establishments, etc.) decided to launch an attack on me to discredit and ridicule the messenger (me). By the COVID era, the cancel crowd was in full swing, trying their best to silence me for suggesting that real food could transform lives. Apparently, cheering for sunlight, movement, fresh air, and building a strong and resilient immune system over their alternative was too much for some!

The MAHA Commission report nods to this reality: certain industries profit when we're unwell, thriving on a cycle of chronic illness. But MAHA can flip this script. By choosing vibrant, whole foods, we can take charge of our health, naturally reducing reliance on those systems—while always respecting that some conditions need specialized care. It's empowerment, not rebellion, and I kept cooking, sharing, connecting, and smiling through the noise.

Let's make this clear: MAHA is for everyone. It's the single mom slow-cooking a nourishing broth to be turned into a delicious soup that can then be frozen in batches to save time during the week, the dad teaching his kids to crack and whisk eggs at the kitchen bench, the couple savoring a simple but heartwarming roast. It's you, wherever you are, choosing to nourish your body and soul. Here's the MAHA Manifesto to light your way:

- **Nourish boldly**: Fill your plate with real, whole foods that fuel your life.
- **Connect deeply**: Share meals, stories, and laughter with those you love.
- **Thrive freely**: Own your health, one delicious choice at a time.

MAHA is a glorious adventure, a chance to rediscover the joy of real food and real connection. It's not about rules or guilt; it's about progress. You can start with one meal a week to begin steering your health ship in a different direction or go all in 100 percent now. There is no magic pill for everyone, as every person's situation is different. I know people who have gone all in, thrown everything out of their pantry, and decided that this moment IS IT! And I have met families that have slowly incorporated these ideas over the span of a few months, ever so gently and slowly, as they didn't want to upset their families with such a massive change all at once. The choice is yours, and only you can discover what is best for you and your situation. My only piece of advice on this is to be flexible, and if guilt, shame, or frustration appear along your journey, let them go, as every day is a new day to reset. So, as a starting point, you may like to gather your loved ones, fire up the stove, and taste the difference. To get you going, try these two simple dishes, perfect for beginners and bursting with MAHA's nutrient-dense ethos:

- **Classic Scrambled Eggs**: Whisk up a handful of farm-fresh eggs, cook low and slow, and serve with a sprinkle of sea salt. It's protein-packed comfort that's ready in minutes.
- **Pan Fried Fish with Broccomole**: Simply pan fry some spanking fresh fish of your choice, whether it be wild salmon, sardines, or some subtle white fish—omega-3 superstars—with a good side of avocado guacamole with the added punch of some broccoli folded through it and a squeeze of lemon. Affordable, delicious, and a nod to the underrated gems of the sea.

These recipes are your first step into MAHA, proof that health starts in the kitchen, no matter your budget or skill level.

So, grab a pan, pick a recipe, and start your MAHA journey today. With Bobby's vision, the MAHA community's passion, and a sprinkle of kitchen magic, we'll make America *and Australia* healthy again. One bite, one meal, one healthier you.

CHAPTER 2

Getting into the Spirit of MAHA

Picture this: It's a Saturday evening, the kitchen's alive with the sizzle of burger patties on the stove or outdoor grill, kids are giggling as they pick some fresh herbs, and your favorite tune is playing in the background. The aroma of real food—honest, nourishing, straight-from-the-earth—fills the air. You sit down to a meal that's not just delicious but makes you feel *alive*. That's the spirit of MAHA, a joyful adventure that starts with one meal and grows into a lifestyle you love. Whether you're a busy parent, a curious beginner, or someone craving more energy, MAHA invites you to rediscover the magic of cooking and eating well. It's not about overhauling your life overnight—even though some do love to jump right into the deep end, whereas others will slowly and thoughtfully change their path—it's all about taking that first step, savoring the moment, and letting health follow.

The MAHA journey begins with a simple choice: cook one meal a week (or many more) that nourishes your body and soul. Maybe it's a hearty soup that warms everyone up, or a quick protein-rich salad. The beauty is in the progress, not perfection. So, how do you get into the spirit of MAHA? It's easier than you think. Start with these three steps:

- **Pick one meal**: Choose a simple recipe out of the book that tickles your fancy, and commit to cooking it this week. It could be a weeknight dinner or a relaxing Sunday breakfast.
- **Make it a moment**: Invite family or friends to join in—kids can stir, partners can chop, or you can vibe solo with music on. Cooking's more fun when it's shared.
- **Savor the win**: After eating, notice how you feel that day and even the day after. Do you have more energy? Are you in a happier mood? Jot it down or share it with your crew. That's MAHA in action.

Don't let worries about lack of time or skill stop you. A MAHA meal can be ready in five to twenty minutes, and you don't need to be a pro—some of my best dishes started as happy accidents! To keep the spark alive, you might like creating a "MAHA night" each week, where you test a new recipe or tweak an old favorite with a fresh herb. Get the kids involved—my own learned to love cooking by cracking eggs and chopping avocado for a guacamole. If you're stuck, flip through this book or think back to a dish your family loves, then give it a MAHA twist with whole ingredients.

Speaking of community, let's have a chat about keeping the MAHA spirit alive. Life can be hectic at times, with work, school runs, and endless to-do lists, but a single meal can ground you. Without getting too woo-woo, try making cooking a ritual. Once upon a time, food was the ultimate priority for humans for survival and was celebrated when the hunting and gathering fed the tribe or village. Some ideas that may resonate could be to light a candle, put on a playlist of your favorite music or listen to an inspiring podcast when you are cooking, and when it is time to share the meal, tell stories at the table and make it a place of inspiring ideas and conversation. If you slip up and grab takeaway, no worries—MAHA's about progress, not guilt. Reflect on what works; maybe the kids loved the burgers, or the soup stretched to lunch. You can even start keeping a journal of your MAHA moments or share them with friends and family to spread the vibe. One of the things that the MAHA movement stresses is that even small changes add up. The simple act of choosing whole real food over processed ones can contribute to big, positive health outcomes. Ultimately, every meal that we cook creates a new reality for ourselves and our loved ones. We are building beautiful memories, strengthening connections and supporting communities, and owning our well-being.

CHAPTER 3

Shopping

Imagine wandering through a bustling farmers' market, the air alive with the scent of fresh herbs and the chatter of growers proud of their craft. You spot a stall piled high with vibrant fruit and vegetables, another offering grass-fed ground beef at a steal, and a fishmonger touting fresh sardines, omega-3 gold for a fraction of the price. This is the MAHA shopping adventure: sourcing high-quality, nutrient-dense ingredients that don't break the bank, all while connecting with the people who bring food to your table. Whether you're a busy parent or a health enthusiast, MAHA makes shopping an exciting step toward vibrant health, one local find at a time.

Shopping MAHA-style is about quality, not cost. But you don't need a fat wallet to eat well. From farmers' markets to co-ops, regenerative farms to your local butcher, there are countless ways to source ingredients that nourish. Fifteen years ago, when I started my health journey, I learned this firsthand. A chance chat with a butcher led me to affordable offal, packed with vitamins I'd been missing. This is what MAHA's all about: finding the best you can, wherever you are.

Here's how to start your MAHA shopping adventure:

- **Explore local sources**: Visit a farmers' market or join a community co-op. Online, search for regenerative farms delivering grass-fed meat or sustainable seafood. Ask your butcher about secondary cuts or your fishmonger for what is budget friendly and fresh . . . it may not be something you are familiar with, but that is why the adventure can be so fun and rewarding.
- **Build relationships**: Chat with growers or suppliers. A friendly question—"What's fresh today?"—can lead to tips on budget buys or seasonal gems. These connections make MAHA personal and fun.

- **Shop smart**: Plan meals around what's local and in-season—cabbage in winter, zucchini and tomatoes in summer. Buy in bulk (split a cow/lamb share with friends and family) or stock up on jarred fish. Eggs, ground meat, and greens are wallet-friendly staples. If your budget allows, you may wish to invest in a large freezer to not only store bulk produce but to store bulk cooking also.
- **Become a recipe detective:** I can't tell you how important and fun it is to realize that every ingredient in the world can be turned into a delicious meal, because when you start exploring cultures and cuisines from around the world, you find they have tried and tested these foods to the point of culinary mastery.

Budget doesn't mean boring. Some of the cheapest ingredients are MAHA superstars. Ground beef, like in **Thai Ground Beef with Basil**, delivers protein and iron. Jarred sardines, as in **Sardine Pâté**, are omega-3 powerhouses that can cost less than a coffee. Offal, featured in **Offal Burger Patties**, is a nutrient bomb; think liver for vitamin A or heart for CoQ10. Cabbage, the hero of **Cabbage and Bacon Soup**, is budget friendly and goes a long way. These ingredients aren't just affordable; they're the backbone of meals that make you feel unstoppable.

To make it easy, here's a **MAHA Shopping List** template to guide you:

- **Proteins**: Eggs, ground beef and secondary cuts of grass-fed beef, sardines, cheaper species of fresh fish, offal/organ meats, game, free range pork and chicken.
- **Fats**: extra-virgin olive oil, coconut oil, tallow, free range lard, grass-fed butter/ghee, duck fat.
- **Produce**: Seasonal greens, cabbage, root veggies, herbs.
- **Pantry**: Sea salt, spices, jarred fish, good-quality vinegars, coconut aminos, tamari.
- **Garden:** Planting fresh herbs every week, and perhaps cherry tomatoes, cucumbers.

Try this: next time you're at a market, ask a farmer about their favorite veggie or a butcher for a deal on ground meat. You might score a recipe tip or a discount. One of my favorite MAHA moments was finding a local grower who sold me a box of "ugly" veggies, perfectly tasty and half the price. Those connections, those finds, are what make shopping a joy, not a chore.

A few tips to keep the adventure going: Plan your shopping with a loose menu in mind, but stay open to surprises. Freeze extra meat or cheap fresh fish for quick meals later on for the weeks ahead. (You are more likely to cook nutrient-dense food if you have it on hand.) If you're on a tight budget, prioritize one MAHA ingredient per week, like eggs or ground meat, and build around it. So, grab your reusable bag, hit the market, and start exploring. Shopping MAHA-style isn't just about filling your fridge; it's about filling your life with health, connection, and flavor.

CHAPTER 4

Cleaning Out the Pantry

Your kitchen pantry is more than a cupboard, it's the heart of your MAHA journey, a treasure trove of ingredients that fuel vibrant health. But if it's stocked with processed snacks and inflammatory oils, it's probably holding you back. Cleaning out your pantry is a powerful reset, a chance to remove what doesn't serve you and embrace whole, nourishing staples that make every meal a step toward well-being. This isn't about deprivation; it's about excitement, swapping out the junk for flavors that sing.

When I started my health journey fifteen years ago, my pantry was full of the normal staples that most people have: vegetable oils, sugary cereals, and packets with some pretty interesting ingredients listed on the labels. Clearing it out felt so, so good. For me and many others, this is really when the dedication and commitment rings true that we have made a heartfelt decision to change. The MAHA Commission's report echoes this: ultra-processed foods and seed oils drive chronic illness, while whole foods heal. A MAHA pantry sets you up to cook with confidence, knowing every ingredient is a choice for vitality. Let's make it happen with a straightforward plan.

Here's how to clean out your pantry, MAHA-style:

- **Take stock**: Pull everything out and check labels. Look for seed and vegetable oils (canola, soybean, sunflower), processed snacks, high carb cereals, and sugary spreads. These are often high in omega-6 fats, which can spark inflammation, or loaded with additives that sap energy and can cause some serious health issues. The old saying holds true: if the label has words you don't understand, then it is probably better off not in your pantry or your body.
- **Clear the decks**: Donate unopened items to a food bank, share with

friends, or phase out opened goods gradually. No guilt—MAHA's about progress.

- **Restock with MAHA staples**: Replace seed oils with olive and coconut oils, tallow, duck fat, and ghee (if you can tolerate dairy). Swap processed seasonings for sea salt and spices like turmeric or cumin. Add different quality vinegars for a splash of acidity to dishes. These are the building blocks of meals that nourish.

Budget shouldn't stop you. Rendering your own tallow from butcher scraps is cheaper than store-bought oils. A jar of sea salt or small purchases of organic spices lasts months. Start small—swap one item, like canola for olive oil, and build from there. My first MAHA pantry moment was tossing out a dusty bottle of vegetable oil and sizzling fish in olive oil instead. The flavor was a wake-up call.

A few tips to keep your pantry thriving: start with one or two staples, like olive oil and sea salt, and add as you go. Buy spices in bulk or share with friends to save cash. Check your pantry monthly to stay MAHA-aligned, tossing anything that sneaks back in. If you're short on space, prioritize multi-use items—tallow for cooking, vinegar for dressings.

CHAPTER 5

The Beautiful Craft of Cooking

Cooking really is a magical experience. It is alchemy that we can create daily, by taking some simple ingredients and preparing them in a wonderful manner, and the end result is much, much more than what we started with. It is a craft, an art form, and an act of beauty that anyone can master. It is an adventure that arouses all our senses. Think of a curry that is simmering and the aromas that tantalize our sense of smell. It is the bacon sizzling in a pan that our ears are highly attuned to hearing. Our eyes are captivated by nature's vibrancy when we look at a colorful salad gently coated in a glorious dressing. Our taste buds are stimulated by the balance of salt, acid, spice, and fat, and our bodies are warmed and nourished by the wonderful soup in our bowls. I know this might sound a little woo-woo for some; however, I encourage and invite you to explore this way of looking at cooking at home, as it not only can open up our senses, but can go even deeper and open up our hearts and minds is such a profound way. Some would say that this is where true health emanates and MAHA comes alive.

Cooking is the heart of MAHA, transforming the whole foods we've sourced and stocked into meals that can fuel our well-being. The MAHA Commission's report underscores this: nutrient-dense foods like fish, meat, and greens, cooked with intention, can push back against chronic illness. You don't need to be a master chef, you just need the intention and curiosity to be open to learning a new craft. Whether this is your first rodeo or you are a confident home cook, it really is about a few techniques, a spark of curiosity, and a willingness to dive in. MAHA's here to guide you, making cooking an adventure that's as rewarding as it is delicious.

Here are three techniques to kickstart your MAHA kitchen:

- **Roast for richness**: Toss veggies or meat with a healthy fat of your choice, such as olive oil or tallow, sea salt, and herbs, then let the oven deepen their flavors. Think golden crispy pork belly or caramelized sweet potatoes.

- **Braise for comfort**: Slow-cook cuts like short ribs in broth until they're tender and succulent. It's a low-effort technique with big results.
- **Season with flair**: A pinch of spice, a dash of lemon, or a sprinkle of herbs can transform a dish. Trust your palate and experiment.

Forget perfection—a little overcooked or slightly crispy edges are part of the fun. MAHA's about progress, not flawlessness. Cooking's a moment to connect with your food, your loved ones, and yourself, turning the kitchen into health's starting line.

To set you up, here's a **MAHA Kitchen Toolkit**:

- A cast-iron skillet: For searing, roasting, or frying.
- A good-quality sharp knife: Makes chopping a breeze and much safer.
- A wooden spoon, stainless tongs, and cutting board: Timeless essentials.
- A large oven tray: Perfect for roasting anything.
- An extra-large pot: A kitchen staple for making bone broth and soups in bulk.

With these tools and your MAHA pantry, you're ready to create meals that rival any takeout. The MAHA community is proof—families everywhere are trading fast food for home-cooked dishes that spark health and happiness.

I want to share with you a few tips that I have seen work for so many people over the years that will help on your MAHA journey. Starting with one recipe that you like and cooking it a few times over a few weeks will build your confidence in the kitchen. I like to invite you to play with flavors and ingredients, as some items can be out of season or sold out/not available for a variety of reasons, which is no reason to not attempt a recipe. Instead, you can swap out one herb for another like cilantro for mint, basil for parsley, or you can substitute beef for lamb, duck for chicken, fish for shrimp, etc. For busy days, prep ingredients ahead of time or choose one-pot dishes that are simple to create, like soups and braises.

CHAPTER 6

Ancestral Diets

Imagine a time when meals came straight from the land—wild salmon from icy rivers, grass-fed beef from rolling hills, berries straight from the wild. These ancestral diets, rooted in local, seasonal, whole foods, kept people strong, sharp, and free from the chronic diseases we face today. A century ago, Dr. Weston A. Price crisscrossed the globe with his wife, discovering that traditional diets fueled vibrant health, while processed foods and modern approaches to diet brought illness. His findings are, for me, the backbone of MAHA, a call to eat real food like our ancestors to reclaim our well-being. This isn't about turning back the clock—it's about blending timeless wisdom with modern ease to make America and Australia healthy again.

Price's 1930s research revealed a powerful truth. From Pacific Islanders eating fish and coconut to Swiss herders thriving on local ingredients, traditional diets varied but shared key traits: whole foods, eating animals from the land and oceans or waterways in a nose-to-tail way, including organ meats, and of course seasonal fruits and vegetables growing locally. Pretty simple, right? These communities had no trace of diabetes, heart disease, or obesity, conditions the MAHA Commission's report ties to ultra-processed foods and other lifestyle factors. When processed goods like white flour and refined sugar crept in, health faltered. MAHA draws on this wisdom, inviting us all to choose nutrient-dense foods that echo our ancestors' plates, from broth to fermented vegetables like sauerkraut, to rebuild our vitality.

MAHA makes ancestral eating practical for today's kitchens. You don't need to hunt your own game or forage in the wild (unless you want to); instead you can prioritize grass-fed meat, wild-caught fish, and pesticide-free fruits and veggies whenever possible.

Let's clear up a myth: ancestral eating isn't a one-size-fits-all rulebook. Price found diversity everywhere—Mediterranean diets rich in olive oil and seafood, Inuit meals of seal and quite a lot of fat, African diets of raw milk, blood, and meat. I like to think that MAHA encapsulates this, encouraging you to choose what's local and seasonal. In Australia, that might mean some kangaroo or barramundi; in America, bison or wild salmon. The focus is quality foods packed with nutrients like vitamin A in liver, omega-3s in salmon, or probiotics in kraut. These are what I and many others believe are the building blocks of health.

Here are four recipes to bring ancestral eating to your table, each nutrient-dense and inspired by Price's discoveries:

- **Chicken Liver Parfait**: Blend liver with fat and herbs for a creamy, vitamin-rich spread. Perfect on veggies or gluten-free toast, it's an ancestral powerhouse.
- **Turmeric Kraut**: Ferment cabbage with turmeric and salt for a tangy, gut-healthy condiment. It's traditional preservation, cheap and vibrant.
- **Wild Salmon with Minted Pea and Lemon Broth**: Poach salmon in a light, lemony broth with peas. Omega-3-packed and full of flavor.
- **Lamb, Mint, and Rosemary Patties**: Grill grass-fed ground lamb with herbs for juicy, protein-rich patties. Simple, ancestral, and a crowd-pleaser.

These dishes make ancestral eating accessible, delicious, modern, and health-giving. A few tips to eat like your ancestors: start with one ancestral food, like wild caught fish or grass-fed beef/lamb, and build from there. Use Chapter 3's sourcing tips for quality ingredients and Chapter 4's pantry for fats and ferments. If organs feel too bold, mix them into burger patties starting at 90 percent ground meat and 10 percent ground organ meat. The MAHA Commission's focus on nutrient-dense foods reminds us: this is the path to give us the best opportunity to sidestep chronic illness. Your kitchen is where this journey starts, one nourishing ancestral bite in the modern world at a time.

Ancestral eating is about more than food; it's about rooting yourself in wisdom to grow a healthier future. It's the warmth of a bone broth, the satisfaction of a perfecting a delicious liver pate, the zing of homemade or store-bought kraut. MAHA makes it yours, merging Price's discoveries with today's possibilities. So, fire up your stove, channel your roots, and eat for vitality.

CHAPTER 7

Foods to Cut Down or Remove

Your MAHA journey is about filling your plate with goodness, through nutrient-dense meals that will spark energy and joy. But to make space for that vibrancy, it's worth eyeing foods that might drag you down. Processed carbs, seed and vegetable oils, and excess sugar can reduce your stamina, cloud your mind, and fuel the chronic illnesses flagged by the MAHA Commission's report. This isn't about ditching your favorites forever or chasing strict diets. It's a gentle invitation and exploration to see how you feel when you ease up on these culprits and celebrate real, natural foods. I am here to show you how, with swaps that keep every bite delicious and satisfying.

The MAHA Commission's report is clear: ultra-processed foods, loaded with refined carbs and inflammatory oils, drive obesity, diabetes, and more. Cutting back can unlock better sleep, sharper focus, or just a lighter step. It's not about guilt or rules. Think of it as a four-week test to discover what your body loves. The MAHA community is doing just that; they are swapping processed snacks for real unadulterated foods and feeling the difference. You don't need to overhaul everything; one small change, like skipping the soda, can start the shift.

Here are three foods to consider reducing, with easy swaps to keep things tasty:

- **Processed carbs (e.g., white bread, pasta)**: These lack nutrients and can spike blood sugar. Try lettuce wraps or zucchini noodles for a fresh alternative.
- **Seed oils (e.g., canola, soybean)**: High in omega-6, they may stir inflammation. Swap for olive and coconut oils or tallow and ghee/butter, flavorful and nourishing, as noted in Chapter 4.
- **Excess sugar (e.g., candy, soft drinks)**: It disrupts energy and gut health. Opt for a drizzle of honey

or small amounts of fresh fruit for natural sweetness.

Pick one or more, cut back for fourteen days to a month, and notice how you feel—maybe more energized or less bloated. If you're wedded to your morning toast, ease in with gluten-free bread/toast (there are many recipes in this book or a good-quality store-bought option, but read the labels) or pair it with avocado and eggs. MAHA's about flexibility, not sacrifice. Cravings can be tough, but leaning on nutrient-dense foods from Chapter 6, like salmon or meat, makes it easier. The MAHA Commission's push for whole foods shows why: these swaps crowd out processed traps, boosting health without the struggle.

Here are three recipes to replace those foods with MAHA-friendly alternatives, each vibrant and health-giving:

- **Burger Bowl**: Layer ground beef, avocado, and greens in a bowl, no bun needed. It's a protein-packed, grain-free spin on a classic, perfect for any meal.
- **Cucumber and Avocado Salad with Ginger and Sesame**: Toss cucumber and avocado with an olive oil–based sesame-ginger dressing. It's low carb, refreshing, and quick, and you can add in some smoked or jarred fish or leftover roast pork or chicken.
- **Jaffa Truffles**: Mix cocoa and orange oil for a low-sugar treat. These bites satisfy without the sugar roller-coaster.

These dishes prove you can skip processed foods and still love your meals. They're the kind of recipes MAHA families are embracing, from kitchen to kitchen.

A few tips to make it stick: Start with one swap, like oil or a snack. Check labels for sneaky sugars or dodgy oils in dressings. If you're tied to a comfort food, try a MAHA version listed in this book. Stock your Chapter 4 pantry with some organic nuts and seeds and your fridge with cooked meats and boiled eggs for quick wins. The MAHA Commission notes that whole foods reduce reliance on systems thriving on illness, as we hinted in Chapter 1, while respecting medical needs. Your choices here are your power—use them to feel your best.

Reducing these foods isn't about missing out—it's about gaining vitality, clarity, and joy. It's the crunch of a fresh salad, the satisfaction of a burger bowl, the delight of fresh fruit that's kind to your body. MAHA's got your back, making every swap a step toward thriving.

CHAPTER 8

Organic, Pesticide-Free, and Regenerative Farming Practices

Your MAHA journey will fill your kitchen with vibrant meals, from sizzling steaks to fresh, protein-packed salads, proving food is one of the foundations of well-being. But health is more than what's on your plate, it's a tapestry of choices that nourish body, mind, and some may even say . . . soul.

This chapter is all about exploring some of the most powerful tools for your MAHA adventure: prioritizing where and when it is possible to choose organic or pesticide-free produce over conventionally grown, as well as wild-caught sustainable seafood over questionable aquaculture practices, and to support regenerative farmers over feedlot options. These choices echo the MAHA Commission's call for real whole foods, which can offer physical and emotional benefits. Let's dive into this a little deeper.

ORGANIC, PESTICIDE-FREE FRUIT AND VEG: NATURE'S FINEST

A century ago, nearly all food was organic, free from synthetic pesticides, grown in harmony with the land. Today, choosing organic or pesticide-free fruit and vegetables is a return to that purity. The MAHA Commission highlights environmental toxins, like pesticides, as drivers of chronic illness, noting their links to everything from gut issues to neurological concerns. Organic produce sidesteps these chemicals, delivering nutrient-dense carrots, apples, or berries that taste like the earth intended. Pesticide-free options, often found at farmers' markets (see Chapter 3), are just as good, grown without harmful sprays, often by small-scale growers who care not only about you the customer but the health of the soil of which they are the stewards.

Why does it matter? Organic veggies are richer in antioxidants and minerals, studies show, and free from residues that disrupt your body's balance. They're not always perfect-looking—expect a wonky zucchini or a speckled apple, but that's the beauty of real food. Budget-wise, prioritize the "dirty dozen" (e.g., spinach, berries) for organic, as they seem to carry the most pesticide load, and then you can save on "clean fifteen" (e.g., avocados, onions) if needed as these seem not to be as heavily affected if not grown organically. A MAHA tip: Wash all produce in filtered water if possible with a splash of apple cider vinegar to remove as much unwanted nasties as possible. By choosing organic or pesticide-free, you're voting for health and supporting farmers who defy industrial norms, just like the MAHA community champions.

NUTS AND SEEDS: TINY POWERHOUSES

Nuts and seeds are compact, nutrient-dense, and versatile. Think almonds packed with vitamin E, chia seeds bursting with omega-3s, or pumpkin seeds loaded with magnesium. A century ago, these were pantry staples, unprocessed and free from the additives found in many modern versions. The MAHA Commission's focus on whole foods aligns here: nuts and seeds offer healthy fats and minerals that support heart health, brain function, and energy, countering the processed snacks we trimmed in Chapter 7. Personally, I love nuts and seeds, but I use them sparingly as I don't think we would have ever consumed them in large quantities as they would have been seasonal, so a little goes a long way.

Choose raw or lightly roasted nuts and seeds, ideally organic to avoid pesticide residues. Soak them overnight (called activating them) to boost digestibility, a trick our ancestors knew well. Budget-conscious? Buy in bulk or stick to affordable options like sunflower seeds. Sprinkle them on salads, blend a little into smoothies, or snack on a handful for a quick boost.

WILD-CAUGHT FISH VS. FARMED FISH: THE OCEAN'S TRUTH

Fish and seafood are MAHA superstars, as they are rich in omega-3s and other powerful nutrients that fight inflammation and boost brain health. But not all fish are equal. Wild-caught fish and seafood, like salmon, shrimp, or sardines, swim free in oceans or rivers, eating natural diets that make them nutrient powerhouses, just as nature intended. On the other hand, farmed fish and other seafood, while not all bad, often come with caveats—crowded pens, synthetic feeds, and antibiotics can lower their nutritional value and harm ecosystems. Some farms do better, using sustainable practices, but wild-caught remains the gold standard. I appreciate the work that US Chef Andrew Gruel has been doing to help inform about this topic over the last decade.

Why choose wild? Wild salmon, as in **Wild Salmon Curry**, delivers more omega-3s and fewer contaminants than most farmed versions. Sardines, a budget-friendly gem, are almost always wild-caught and sustainable. Check labels or ask your fishmonger—Chapter 3's sourcing tips apply here. If farmed fish is your only option, look for certifications (for example, from the Aquaculture Stewardship Council (ASC)), or ask about feed and water quality. By prioritizing wild-caught, you're supporting fishermen and -women, who work against industrial tides and toward nourishing your body with the ocean's best.

REGENERATIVE FARMING: HEALING THE LAND

Regenerative farming—as the name suggests—regenerates nature in the most beautiful and helpful ways and I believe is one of MAHA's secret weapons. It is a way to grow food that heals the soil, sequesters carbon, and produces nutrient-dense crops and meats and that to me sounds like a win, win, win for all. Unlike industrial agriculture, which depletes the earth with monocrops and chemicals, regenerative practices rotate crops, allow animals to graze naturally, and help rebuild ecosystems. Joel Salatin of Polyface Farms has been a pioneer here for decades, raising grass-fed cattle, pastured poultry, and vibrant produce in Virginia, proving that farming can nourish both people and planet. His methods, blending tradition and innovation, echo the organic purity of one hundred years ago, when synthetic fertilizers didn't exist.

One of the main concerns raised by The MAHA Commission's report is how environmental toxins tie in with these farming practices: the good news is that there is a solution that exists right now, and that solution is that regenerative farms do avoid pesticides and chemicals, producing beef, chicken, eggs, or veggies that are cleaner and richer in nutrients. When we choose to support and buy from these farms, via markets, co-ops, or online, it supports the growers who have turned their backs on the industrial system and dedicated their lives to doing what they believe is right for the earth, the animals, and for YOU. It's not always cheap, but sharing a cow or buying seasonal produce can help keep costs down. I like to think that every purchase is a vote for a healthier earth, aligning with MAHA's mission to reduce reliance on systems that harm us, as noted in Chapter 1, and for that I celebrate their tenacity. Let's hope that, in the future, these practices are supported by the government to help them flourish, which would bring the prices down as they have done for Big Agriculture in the past.

PLANTING AN HERB GARDEN: SOIL, KIDS, AND SOUL

Nothing says MAHA like getting your hands in the dirt, and planting an herb garden is the perfect way to start. It's a family affair; kids love digging, planting, and watching basil or mint sprout. A century ago, nearly every backyard had herbs, fresh and organic by default. Today, a small pot on a windowsill or a garden patch brings that tradition back. Herbs like parsley, thyme, or rosemary, grown pesticide-free, add flavor and nutrients (think vitamin C in parsley) to your MAHA meals.

The health benefits go beyond the plate. Digging in soil exposes you to beneficial microbes, boosting immunity and mood, and science backs this "dirt therapy." You might go to Dr. Maya Klein's book, *The Dirt Cure*, for an eye-opening read. For kids, it's a lesson in patience and care, plus a screen-free joy that builds emotional resilience. Emotionally, gardening grounds you, easing stress and connecting you to the earth. Start simple: grab pots, organic soil, and seeds from a local nursery. Let kids water or pick leaves for dishes like **Hasselback Sweet Potatoes**. Our herb garden at home is ever growing. We grow Japanese shiso leaf, Vietnamese mint, Thai basil, wasabi leaf, tarragon, chervil, dill, oregano, kaffir lime leaves, and a whole lot more . . . we absolutely love it. A MAHA tip: compost veggie scraps to feed your garden, closing the loop.

SUPPORTING ETHICAL FARMERS AND FISHERMEN

Choosing organic produce, wild fish, or regenerative meats means supporting farmers and fishermen who go against the grain. These folks—small-scale growers, sustainable fishermen and -women, regenerative ranchers, work hard to defy industrial systems that prioritize profit over health. A century ago, all food came from such hands, grown or caught with care. Today, every dollar you spend at a market or co-op (Chapter 3) is a nod to their grit.

The emotional reward? Knowing your choices uplift communities and protect the land. Health-wise, you're eating cleaner, nutrient-rich food. Budget-wise, prioritize one ethical purchase a week (such as wild sardines or organic greens) and build from there, and you can choose to stop supporting multinational food companies by just opting out of their products. Remember, they can't force you to consume their products! Connect with producers, as we discussed in Chapter 3, to learn their stories. It's a MAHA win: you thrive, they thrive, the earth thrives.

These recipes in the book tie your MAHA tools organic produce, grass-fed meat, wild seafood, nuts and seeds, garden herbs to the kitchen, making health a daily delight.

CHAPTER 9

Meal Prep Planning and Cooking in Bulk

MAHA's all about making health simple, and meal prep planning is your secret weapon to save time, stress, and cash while keeping your kitchen humming with nutrient-dense meals. Cooking in bulk and treating recipes as flexible guidelines lets you embrace the MAHA lifestyle, even on the busiest days. Whether you're a parent juggling school runs or just want more time to enjoy life, these strategies, paired with the recipes in this book, make healthy eating effortless and adaptable.

PLAN SMART, SAVE TIME

Start by picking a prep day, Saturday or Sunday works for many. Choose two to three recipes from this book, like **Pulled Pork, Slow Cooked Brisket,** or **Cabbage and Bacon Soup**, that store well and stretch across meals. Check your Chapter 4 pantry and Chapter 3 shopping list, then make a plan: roast veggies and meat one day, simmer a soup the next. Double the batch—cook enough **Chicken and Vegetable Soup** for dinners and lunches. Use a calendar or app to map your week, factoring in leftovers.

COOK IN BULK, WIN BIG

Bulk cooking is a game-changer. Make a large tray of **Braised Short Ribs** to serve with different sides (salad one night, sweet potatoes another). Soups like **Mexican Beef and Vegetable Soup** freeze beautifully—portion into containers for grab-and-go meals. Invest in glass containers or reusable bags for storage, and label with dates. Bulk cooking saves hours and keeps your fridge stocked with MAHA goodness, ready when hunger strikes.

FLEXIBLE RECIPES, MAHA STYLE

This book's recipes are guides, not rules, so swap out ingredients based on what's cheaper or available. Can't find wild salmon? Then use jarred salmon, sardines, tuna, or mackerel. No ground lamb for patties? Then ground beef, turkey, or chicken works. Out of organic cucumber for **Cucumber and Avocado Salad**? Try zucchini or celery. Seasonal or budget buys from Chapter 3's markets or co-ops are perfect—use what's fresh or on sale. This flexibility, rooted in ancestral wisdom (Chapter 6), keeps MAHA accessible. Taste as you go, adjusting spices or herbs from your Chapter 4 pantry to make it yours.

CHAPTER 10

Fussy Eaters

One of the most common questions I have been asked is about fussy eaters. Fussy eaters, whether they are kids or sometimes adults, have been known to make mealtimes a real challenge. So, how do we turn this hurdle into a fun adventure for everyone? First, we grasp that stepping out of our comfort zones to embrace new flavors is a skill that anyone can learn, and with a little patience, our children (and/or partners) will inevitably follow suit. MAHA thrives when everyone at the table can experience the most nutrient-dense meals that are on the table in front of us. By preparing and presenting foods repeatedly, offering ingredients separately for creative control, and involving children in the prep, we can ignite a spark of love for vibrant flavors, making health a family affair.

The key to overcoming fussy eating is persistence. Research shows kids may need ten to fifteen exposures to a new food before accepting it, so don't give up if any of the recipes in this book get a nose-wrinkle at first. Serve them alongside familiar favorites, like **Roast Chicken** (Chapter 5), without pressure as curiosity grows with time. Adults, too, can push past habits; try a new spice from your Chapter 4 pantry, like turmeric in **Turmeric Kraut**, to wake up your palate. MAHA's about exploration, not force, and every small taste is a win. On a personal note, I was a very fussy eater as a child, and then I decided to become a chef, so I had to learn and appreciate all these new ingredients and flavors . . . and now all the things I thought I wouldn't like are my favorite foods to eat, such as oysters, organ meats, mushrooms, and Brussels sprouts.

A game-changer for kids is letting them create their own dishes. Set out ingredients from recipes—think patties, lettuce, avocado, and organic cucumber—on the dinner table. Let them build their own burgers or invent wraps, mixing and matching as they please. This hands-on approach, inspired by these flexible recipes, gives kids control, making new flavors exciting, not daunting. It's budget-friendly too—just use what's on hand or cheaper swaps (e.g., zucchini for cucumber).

Getting kids involved in prep is pure magic. When possible, invite them to pick herbs from your garden, whisk eggs or shape burger patties. This isn't just fun—it builds willingness to try new ingredients. A child who sprinkles sesame seeds on a salad is more likely to taste it. Prep Time also fosters emotional bonds, boosting confidence and joy, much like gardening's benefits. For busy families, even small tasks count—shaking spices or picking basil leaves.

MAHA's fussy-eater strategy is about patience and play. Repeated exposure, creative freedom, and hands-on prep turn "yuck" into "yum."

CHAPTER 11

A Word on Water

Water is essential for life and a foundation for vibrant health. But not all water is equal. Spring water or filtered, fluoride-free and chlorine-free water delivers purity that nourishes our bodies. It sidesteps toxins that the MAHA commissions report alerts us to as health risks. This simple choice can boost energy and support health, by choosing the cleanest and most pure water to amplify our MAHA lifestyle. Whether you're on a tight budget or chasing the best, here are a few reasons why water quality really does matter and how to make it work for you.

Clean water is a health game-changer. Fluoride, added to many tap supplies, may disrupt thyroid function or neurological health, per emerging studies, while chlorine, used to kill bacteria, can irritate skin and gut. The MAHA Commission notes environmental toxins' role in chronic illness, and filtered water can help cut those risks, delivering hydration that supports clear thinking, detoxing, and nutrient absorption. Spring water, straight from natural sources, is the gold standard, often rich in minerals like magnesium, but tap water, properly filtered, is another option.

Budget options make clean water accessible. A countertop filter (e.g., ceramic or carbon-based) can remove fluoride, chlorine, and heavy metals—check for a National Science Foundation (NSF) certification. Pitcher filters are cheaper but less thorough; they're a solid start. If spring water's available, look for local sources or bulk delivery to save. Refill reusable nontoxic bottles at community springs if you're near one, free and pure.

Choosing clean water supports your health and aligns with MAHA's ethos of defying industrial systems, like those adding chemicals to water or food (Chapter 1). It's a nod to a century ago, when water flowed naturally, untainted. The emotional lift? Knowing you're giving your family the best, from a cool glass to a steaming **Pete's Cold and Flu Tea**. The MAHA community, champions this purity, choosing quality over convenience. So, grab a filter, seek a spring, or start small; every sip of clean water is a step toward thriving.

And don't forget you may also wish to use the cleanest water possible for making your broths and boiling your veggies in too.

CHAPTER 12

Protein, Fats, and Lower Carbs

The MAHA journey is about choosing the best foods that can fuel your body that spark long-term vitality, and few do this better than good-quality meat and seafood that contain healthy proteins and fats. These nutrient-dense powerhouses that are celebrated by many doctors that have inspired me, like Dr. Gabrielle Lyon, Dr. Paul Saladino, and Dr. Shawn Baker, help to build strength, sharpen focus, and sustain energy for adults and children alike. Lowering carbohydrate intake without sidelining the vibrant herbs and some fruits and vegetables we enjoy can amplify these benefits, balancing blood sugar and supporting long-term health. It is little wonder why the MAHA Commissions report emphasizes the call for whole foods, urging us to prioritize high-quality proteins and fats over processed carbs. Let's take a deeper look and explore how this simple approach, rooted in ancestral wisdom, can make your family thrive, with flexibility to keep meals delicious and doable.

MEAT AND SEAFOOD: THE BUILDING BLOCKS

Meat and seafood are MAHA's cornerstones, delivering protein that repairs muscles, supports immunity, and fuels growth. A growing number of doctors advocate for and emphasize protein's role in maintaining lean mass, especially as we age, which is key for adults chasing strength or kids building healthy bodies. Grass-fed beef offers iron and B12 for energy and brain health. Wild-caught fish packs omega-3s that fight inflammation and boost cognition. Organ meats, such as liver, brains, heart, and kidneys (Chapter 6), are nutrient bombs—vitamin A, zinc, and more—echoing ancestral diets (Chapter 6).

For kids, protein is vital for growth and focus. A child savoring **Steak and Eggs with Chimmichurri** gets amino acids for muscles and steady energy for school. Seafood, like sardines in **Sardine Pâté**, supports brain development with DHA.

MAHA's budget tips (Chapter 3) make it accessible—ground meats, jarred and smoked fish, and offal are affordable, nutrient-dense choices. Source from farmers' markets or regenerative farms (Chapter 8) for quality, and cook in bulk (Chapter 8) to save time. These proteins aren't just food—they're fuel for a vibrant life.

HEALTHY FATS: NATURE'S ENERGY SOURCE

Healthy fats are MAHA's unsung heroes, providing sustained energy, hormone support, and nutrient absorption. Olive and coconut oil, tallow, butter, and ghee, stocked in your Chapter 4 pantry, are staples. Tallow, used in cooking a steak, is rich in stable saturated fats, perfect for cooking and heart health when paired with whole foods. Extra-virgin olive oil, delivers monounsaturated fats and antioxidants. Avocados and nuts, like sesame seeds, add creamy fats that kids love. Dr. Shawn Baker, a carnivore diet proponent, highlights animal fats' role in satiety and clarity, though MAHA keeps it balanced by including plant-based foods also. Many can benefit from going full carnivore for a few months, as I myself have done, as a basic reset, but it is also worth listening to your body and consulting a health professional if you have any questions or concerns.

For children, fats are critical for brain development and energy. A drizzle of olive oil on some grilled fish or ghee or lard or other healthy fat of choice makes meals satisfying, reducing sugar crashes. Fats also help absorb vitamins from fruits and veggies—think carrots with tallow for vitamin A. Budget-wise, render your own fat (Chapter 4) or buy olive oil in bulk. These fats, free from inflammatory seed oils (Chapter 7), align with the MAHA Commission's whole-food focus, powering your family without processed junk.

LOWERING CARBS: A BALANCED APPROACH

Carbohydrates are not the enemy, as some would have you believe. However, in this modern age, I and many others do believe that we have upped the dose of these in our diet to alarming levels. Simply lowering our carbohydrates intake (without demonizing fruits and vegetables) can help us by stabilizing blood sugar, improving focus, and supporting our metabolic health. The MAHA Commission report links processed carbs to obesity and diabetes. High-carb diets, which alarmingly are recommended by dietary associations around the world, are heavy in breads, grains, and cereals. They spike glucose, leading to energy dips, cravings, and can lead to chronic health issues. By reducing these in your diet, it shifts your body to use fats and proteins for steady energy. For adults, this can mean better weight management and mental clarity, and for kids it can support growth with fewer mood swings. I like the analogy of creating a fire using wood . . . whereas carbohydrates are like kindling (small pieces of wood) and to keep the fire going, we need to continually keep putting more and more kindling on the fire to stop it from going out (which is how many people in the western world eat), whereas the other option is to put a big fat log on the fire and it will burn slow and steady, without the need to add more large logs so often. Think of the big fat logs as good-quality fat and proteins from well-sourced animals.

Fruits and veggies remain MAHA stars—organic berries or pesticide-free greens—offer fiber, vitamins, and flavor. The goal is to cut or reduce refined carbs (pasta, cereals) and moderate starchy ones (sweet potatoes, etc.), favoring nutrient-dense options. Italian sausage with greens instead of grain-filled bread saves carbs while keeping kids full. For adults, **Sweet Potato Wedges with Smoked Paprika** in moderation add balance to a lovely roast piece of meat or grilled fish. Kids might start with smaller portions of veggies paired with protein like **Roast Chicken** (Chapter 5) to avoid sugar spikes. MAHA's flexible recipes let you swap high-carb sides for low-carb options if budgets or seasons dictate.

The benefits are clear: adults feel sharper, kids stay focused, and everyone avoids the processed traps the MAHA Commission warns against. Repeated exposure helps kids embrace these meals, especially if they can help out in the preparation in some way.

BRINGING IT TOGETHER

Focusing on meat, seafood, and healthy fats, with fewer carbs, is MAHA's recipe for thriving. These choices—grass-fed meats, wild game, free-range poultry, wild fish, olive oil, and lower carb vegetables and fruits can fuel your body, align with Chapter 3's sourcing and Chapter 8's regenerative ethos, and make health simple.

CHAPTER 13

Gut Health and Fermented Foods

One thing that really has taken hold for me over the last fifteen years is the realization that our gut is the cornerstone of our health, as it drives digestion, immunity, and even our mood. The mission of MAHA is to nourish holistically, and it shines here with three powerful tools: eliminating toxins by choosing pesticide-free produce, slowly adding some fermented foods to our diet, and including prebiotics from real foods. As highlighted in the MAHA commission's report, environmental toxins like pesticides are one of the culprits of this chronic health debacle in which many find themselves, but luckily, a thriving gut can fight back. By choosing pesticide-free produce and starting to include fermented foods like sauerkraut in your diet, you're creating a healthier you, with science-backed benefits that can make every bit a step toward vitality.

The pesticides that are sprayed on conventional produce can disrupt your gut microbiome, with studies linking chemicals like glyphosate to a raft of issues such as inflammation, bloating, and even autoimmune issues. So, it may be wise to opt for spray-free produce and organic fruits and vegetables over these conventional ones whenever possible.

Found at places like Whole Foods, farmers' markets, or co-ops, pesticide-free veggies can be budget-friendly; grab seasonal or "imperfect" ones to save. Pair with healthy fats like olive oil in **Pan-Fried Fish with Broccomole** to boost nutrient absorption, powering your gut for energy and immunity across ages.

Fermented foods are gut-health heroes, delivering probiotics that can help to balance your microbiome. Options like **Turmeric Kraut** or kimchi provide live bacteria, easing digestion, curbing inflammation, and supporting mental clarity via the gut-brain axis, per a 2021 study on microbial diversity.

Fermented foods and beverages can enhance nutrient uptake, amplifying pesticide-free benefits. Ancestral diets throughout the world leaned on fermented foods like kefir, yogurt, sauerkraut, and kimchi for preservation and health. You may wish to start with a teaspoon daily, building to a tablespoon at mealtimes to avoid tummy troubles by having too much too soon. The good news is that homemade fermented foods are quite cheap to make if wish to go on this adventure, as all you need is cabbage and salt, or you can opt for quality store-bought options as an entry point.

A few words here on how prebiotics from real foods can fuel those good bacteria, tying ferments and spray-free produce together. Garlic, onions, leeks, bananas and many others offer fibers like inulin, boosting digestion and immunity, per a 2019 study showing prebiotics enhance probiotic effects. You can simply indulge in some budget-friendly onions or leeks that shine in dishes like stews, curries and roasts pairing perfectly with **Kraut** for a gut-health double act. This trio of pesticide-free produce, ferments, and prebiotics has shown to transform guts around the world. Pesticide-free veggies shield it, and fermented foods and prebiotics strengthen it. They align with the Commission's vision, reducing reliance on illness-driven systems (Chapter 1).

CHAPTER 14

An Invitation for Further Discovery

Your MAHA journey can and will transform your kitchen, gut, and plate, but true health weaves through every part of life. This final chapter invites you to explore beyond food, diving into practices that nourish body, mind, and spirit. From nature's embrace to rewriting your story, these tools, rooted in curiosity and courage, amplify the MAHA Commission's vision for vibrant living. They're not rules, but as I like to say, "invitations," inspired by the holistic ethos that makes America healthy again. Let's dive into these discoveries, each a step toward a thriving you, with practical tips to make them yours.

SPENDING TIME IN NATURE

Nature is MAHA's ultimate healer, boosting mood, slashing stress, and grounding your body. Studies show just twenty minutes in a park or forest lowers cortisol, enhances immunity, and sharpens focus which benefits adults and kids alike. The MAHA Commission's toxin concerns remind us: nature counters urban overload. A walk in the woods, a picnic by the sea, or barefoot moments on grass (see *earthing*) can recharge you. No forest nearby? A city park or backyard works. Budget-friendly: it's free. Make it a ritual, weekly hikes or sunrise strolls. Nature's not just scenery; it's medicine, reconnecting you to the earth that fuels your MAHA meals. So, step outside, breathe deep, and let the outdoors spark your vitality.

HONORING CIRCADIAN RHYTHMS

We all have an internal clock, known as our circadian rhythm, which governs sleep, energy, and hormones, and MAHA invites you to sync with it. Disrupted rhythms from erratic schedules and overexposure to artificial light can cause our health to suffer. Thankfully, there are some simple solutions to this, including natural light exposure, especially morning sunlight, that helps set our internal clock, which can boost our mood and sleep quality. At night we can dim lights and reduce our screen time.

Practical steps: wake with the sun, eat meals at consistent times, and choose to wind down early. And how cool is this: sunlight is free. For kids, regular bedtimes mimic ancestral patterns. Sip some chamomile tea in the evening to relax. Honoring your rhythm isn't rigid, it's freedom to thrive.

LESS BLUE LIGHT AT NIGHTTIME

Blue light from screens and LEDs tricks your brain into staying awake, disrupting sleep and circadian rhythms. The MAHA Commission's holistic lens supports minimizing this modern toxin. Research shows blue light suppresses melatonin, harming sleep quality and mood for adults and kids. After sunset, cut screen time and use warm lighting—think candles or amber bulbs. Now there are dedicated blue light–blocking options from reading lights to bedside lamps and even ceiling lights. You may have seen people in the biohacking arena wearing blue blocking glasses of an evening, and there are apps like f.lux that dim the blue light from laptops and computers. For kids, you can swap bedtime screens for books. Create a night routine: dim lights and relax. Less blue light means deeper rest and sharper days.

MOVING YOUR BODY JOYFULLY

Movement is MAHA's spark, and it's best when it puts a smile on your face. The MAHA Commission's call for active lifestyles highlights exercise's role in fighting chronic illness. Forget grueling gyms (unless that is your jam); simply dance to your favorite tune, kick a ball with kids, or stroll with a friend. Studies show joyful movement boosts endorphins, heart health, and energy for all ages. Budget-friendly: a walk in the park, a swim in the lake/ocean or pool, or home dance party costs nothing or near to nothing. For kids, games like tag count. Make it fun: try yoga, Pilates, or backyard ball games. Joyful movement isn't a chore; it's play that fuels your MAHA life and PLAY is the key word!

SETTING UP YOUR ROOM FOR SLEEP

A core of the MAHA foundation is to get a great night's sleep, and our bedrooms set the stage. In the MAHA Commission's report, our lifestyle choices including our sleep are tied to our health. Poor rest and sleep can fuel chronic issues. Studies have shown how a dark, cool room can boost melatonin and deepen sleep.

Budget tips: use blackout curtains or an eye mask, earplugs, or a fan for white noise or no noise at all is often best. Clear clutter for calm, store devices elsewhere to cut blue light (see above). For kids, a cozy setup with a story works wonders. You may wish to add a little lavender sprig for relaxation under a pillow or place lavender essential oil on the base of your feet when hopping into bed. Make it a sanctuary: no work, just rest. A MAHA sleep space recharges you for vibrant days.

EMF AWARENESS WITHOUT FEAR

Electromagnetic fields (EMFs) that emanate from our devices such as phones and Wi-Fi routers are a part of modern life for most people; however MAHA invites us to explore mindful awareness on this topic without panic or fear. The MAHA Commission's stance on toxic exposure includes environmental factors, and some studies suggest any high EMF exposure may disrupt stress responses and mess with our sleep.

No need for fear; simple steps reduce exposure. Turn off Wi-Fi at night, keep phones out of bedrooms, or use airplane mode at a bare minimum. You may like to consider using wired headphones instead of Bluetooth headphones and earphones. For kids, limit device time and encourage play. Pair with grounding for balance. MAHA's advice about practical choices and awareness empowers you to live vibrantly, not anxiously.

EARTHING AND GROUNDING

Earthing, which is connecting barefoot to the earth, is MAHA's simple, powerful reset. Studies show contact with soil or grass reduces inflammation, improves sleep, and calms stress by balancing your body's electrical charge. The MAHA Commission's toxin concerns align here: nature counters modern overload. Walk barefoot in a park, garden, or beach, it is free and accessible. For kids, it's play; let them dig and plant herbs with you. The MAHA community loves it and families report calmer moods post-grounding. So, kick off your shoes, feel the earth, and recharge.

SOCIAL CONNECTION

Connection is MAHA's heartbeat, lifting spirits and health. Studies show social bonds, chatting with friends, family dinners, or community events can slash stress and boost longevity, aligning with the MAHA Commission's lifestyle focus. Call a friend, host a MAHA meal, or join a market meet-up. Make it regular, weekly catch-ups or cooking with loved ones. Connection fights isolation, fueling your MAHA journey.

CONSCIOUS BREATHING

Conscious breathing is MAHA's simple, powerful tool to melt stress and restore balance. Deep, intentional breaths activate your parasympathetic nervous system, lowering cortisol and boosting calm. The MAHA Commission's lifestyle focus supports this: stress management counters chronic illness. A basic practice is when you are feeling like you need some calm, inhale for four counts, hold for four, exhale for four to six counts, or simply inhale for four counts and exhale for four counts and repeat. It takes just a minute, anywhere, anytime. Do it before meals to aid digestion or during nature walks for grounding. For kids, make it fun—blow imaginary bubbles or breathe with a story. The great news is that it's free. Regular practice improves focus, sleep, and resilience, benefiting all ages. MAHA's about accessible health; breathing consciously fits busy lives, no gear needed.

COLD THERAPY AND HEAT THERAPY

Cold therapy, like cold showers or ice baths, and heat therapy, such as hot baths or saunas, are MAHA's dynamic duo for health. Studies show cold exposure boosts circulation, reduces inflammation, and lifts mood by spiking endorphins, ideal for adults and teens. A ten- to thirty-second cold shower (free) or a dip in a cool lake or ocean wakes your body, aligning with the MAHA Commission's active lifestyle push. Heat therapy, which can come from warm baths or saunas, relaxes muscles, lowers stress, and improves heart health, per research. An Epsom salt bath or community sauna visit works. Budget tip: hot showers mimic baths. Alternate cold and hot for contrast therapy, always mindful of how hot your bath or shower can get so you don't have it too hot.

MINDFUL LANGUAGE AND REWRITING YOUR STORY

The words we use to describe ourselves, "our story," shapes our reality. I invite you to observe your language, both spoken and internal, and to contemplate rewriting any limiting narratives with curiosity and courage. The MAHA Commission's holistic lens supports this: mental habits impact health as much as diet. If you say, "I'm always tired," you are probably reinforcing that state. You could swap it out for, "I'm finding new energy," and watch your mindset shift. Studies show positive self-talk boosts resilience and lowers stress, benefiting adults and kids modeling your words. Your story, the beliefs about who you are, can trap you in old patterns. MAHA is about pulling those threads: Why do you believe you're "stuck"? Dive deep, question, and rewrite with empowering words.

Practical steps: Journal daily, noting phrases like "I can't" and reframing them to "I'm learning." Speak kindly to yourself, as you would a dear friend. For kids, encourage "I'll have a little to taste" over "I don't like it." Budget-friendly: A notebook costs little, and quiet reflection is free. This isn't fluffy, it's transformative. A MAHA family I know shifted from "we're unhealthy" to "we're growing stronger," sparking better meals and play. Your internal thoughts matter too.

Catch negative loops and redirect with curiosity: "Why do I feel this way?" Courage to rewrite your story creates a new you, aligning with MAHA's empowerment ethos. The Commission's vision of vibrant living thrives here, and some may say that your story and your words ARE your medicine.

Screen time shapes your story too. Doomscrolling drains energy. MAHA urges mindful attention—where focus goes, energy flows. Limit screen times, swapping for play or nature. Curate uplifting content, recipes, health tips, or MAHA community stories. Your story is your power; dive into who you believe you are, question why, and craft a new narrative.

FASTING

Fasting is just the absence of taking in food for a period of time. We all fast between our last meal and our next, which is where the term *breakfast* comes from, as the first meal of the day is usually the longest we have been without any food since the meal before (the day prior). Duration of a fast is really down to the individual and not something that I would recommend to a family to do together, as every person is different. As adults, we generally fast for about ten to twelve hours, depending on your last meal and first meal the next day. Many people now do what is called intermittent fasting, which pushes out their fast to about fourteen to sixteen hours, perhaps one day a week or more. Intermittent fasting isn't for everyone, but you might like to see how you feel by giving a whirl. I personally listen to my body and generally eat good-sized meals once or twice daily, but again, I cannot emphasize this enough: everyone is different and I invite you to be flexible in your approach.

BONE BROTHS

Bone broths are not only the flavor backbone of so many cuisines and recipes, but they are also a nutrient powerhouse that I believe should be celebrated in home kitchens on their MAHA adventure. Every culture and cuisine has some type of bone broth in its repertoire, as I mentioned before about flavor, but when we take a step back and give a nod to our ancestors, it makes perfect sense that our bodies would have such a deep relationship with this humble offering. When a hunt was completed, our ancestors never would have wasted anything from the hunt. The fur would have been utilized, the organ meats shared along with the meat and fat, and the bones were simmered in a vessel with water and whatever other local or traded spices and herbs that were available. Today we now know that bone broths offer so much more than just flavor. They offer nutrients and minerals such as calcium, collagen, gelatine, magnesium, glucosamine, and the list goes on . . . it really is a delicious multivitamin in one recipe. I invite you to view making bone broth as a gift to yourself and your family and friends. We make a large pot every week or so and then chill it and freeze it in glass jars so we have them on hand always. From subtle chicken, aromatic fish, rich pork, and beef broths, they are a foundation in many a MAHA kitchen.

* * *

Let's get into some MAHA recipes in the coming pages.

I do wish to state again that these recipes are to be used as a guide, and that they are not set in stone. Feel free to substitute one herb for another, replace chicken for beef and so on. The recipes are all gluten- and grain-free; however, if you wish to add some rice to your favorite curry, or some sourdough bread to one of your delicious soups for dipping, please feel free. The reason I have excluded grains from this book is that it seems to work best to give the body a nice little reset, as this choice to remove grains for a period of time really forces us to fill our plates with good-quality seafood, meat, and vegetables. I invite you to see how you feel by doing so. I also haven't included any dairy except for butter or ghee as other fat options to cook with in addition to the other healthy fats outlined. The reason for this is many people have dairy sensitivities and grass-fed butter and ghee seem to be the least problematic of the dairy options. If you do not have any problems with including dairy, then please do what feels right for you . . . and if you do, please include the very best quality dairy you can find.

The recipes following will be in chapters such as beef, chicken, seafood, breakfast, treats, drinks, and more.

I invite you to try occasionally cooking what you would consider a dinner recipe to have for breakfast and vice versa, as these are really just labels, and the further we can remove ourselves from any type of labels the more exciting the adventure can be.

PART II
The MAHA Recipes

MAHA BREAKFAST: WHERE THE DAY BEGINS . . . OR WHENEVER YOU LIKE

Mornings at MAHA aren't bound by the clock, they're about gathering around flavors that feel like home. I would love you to picture this . . . a kitchen filled with the aroma of what our grandparents were used to, steak and eggs sizzling in the pan that sets us up for the day's adventures. But here's the beauty of it: at MAHA, any meal can be breakfast, and breakfast can sneak into any time of day. Craving some scrambled eggs with smoked salmon at sunset? Why not? Or the hemp seed muesli as a dessert after dinner. It's all fair game. These recipes draw from the heart of different cultures and cuisines, where food is flexible, shared, and always inviting. Whether you're starting your day with a vibrant spread, choosing to intermittently fast and skip the morning meal altogether, or flipping the script with dinner vibes at dawn, this chapter is your invitation to mix it up. After all, in the kitchen, rules are meant to be deliciously broken.

CLASSIC SCRAMBLED EGGS

SERVES: 2

Prep Time: 5 minutes **Cook Time:** 3–4 minutes

4 organic, free-range eggs
3 tablespoons melted ghee or good-quality animal fat such as tallow, lard, or coconut oil, *divided*
1 tablespoon full-fat coconut milk
Sea salt and freshly ground black pepper
Dulse flakes, *optional*

Tip:

I sometimes finish mine with a touch of extra-virgin truffle oil or olive oil for added depth and richness.

1. Crack the eggs into a large bowl, add 2 tablespoons of the melted ghee or fat and the coconut milk, and whisk to combine. Season well with salt and pepper.
2. Heat the remaining 1 tablespoon of ghee or fat in a nonstick skillet over medium heat. Pour in the egg mixture and cook for about 1½ minutes, gently lifting and pushing the mixture from the edges of the pan toward the center using a wooden spoon or silicone spatula.
3. Remove the skillet from the heat and gently fold the eggs a few times. Let them rest for 30–60 seconds so the residual heat finishes cooking.
4. Divide the scrambled eggs between serving plates. Sprinkle with a pinch of dulse flakes, if using, and serve.

STEAK AND EGGS WITH CHIMICHURRI

SERVES: 2

Prep Time: 5 minutes **Cook Time:** 5 minutes

- **4 (5-ounce/140-g) grass-fed minute steaks**
- **2 tablespoons melted coconut oil or good-quality animal fat, *divided***
- **Sea salt and freshly ground black pepper**
- **4 organic, free-range eggs**
- **Chimichurri (page 247)**

1. Heat an outdoor grill to hot or a large skillet over high heat.
2. Brush the steaks with 1 tablespoon of the coconut oil or animal fat and season with a generous amount of salt and pepper.
3. Cook the steaks for 1–1½ minutes, then flip over and cook for 1 minute on the other side for medium–rare (or cook to your liking). Transfer to a plate and allow to rest for 5 minutes, keeping warm.
4. Heat the remaining oil or fat in a large nonstick skillet over medium heat. Crack in the eggs and fry for 2–2½ minutes until the egg whites are set (or cook to your liking). Season with salt and pepper.
5. Serve the steaks on a platter or plates, top each with a fried egg, and drizzle over the chimichurri.

BACON, TOMATO, AND SPINACH OMELET

SERVES: 4

Prep Time: 10–15 minutes **Cook Time:** 22 minutes (1 minute resting time)

1 tablespoon melted coconut oil or good-quality animal fat, plus extra for greasing
½ yellow onion, finely chopped
2 slices free-range bacon, chopped
6 free-range, organic eggs
Sea salt and freshly ground black pepper
½ bunch spinach (about 3½ ounces / 100 g), stems removed and leaves roughly chopped
6 cherry tomatoes, halved
1 handful arugula leaves

1. Preheat the oven to 400°F (200°C) or 350°F (180°C fan-forced / convection).
2. Heat the coconut oil or fat in a skillet over medium–high heat. Add the onion and cook, stirring occasionally, for 5 minutes, or until translucent. Add the bacon and cook for a further 5 minutes, or until lightly golden. Remove from the heat and allow to cool.
3. Whisk the eggs with a pinch of salt and pepper in a bowl.
4. Grease an ovenproof skillet with a little coconut oil or fat. Scatter over the spinach and cooked onion and bacon mixture in a single layer. Pour over the egg mixture, then arrange the cherry tomatoes on top and press down lightly. Cook the omelet over medium heat for 1 minute, then transfer to the oven for 8–10 minutes until the egg is lightly golden on top and cooked through.
5. Let the omelet rest for a minute in the pan, then top with the arugula and serve.

THAI GROUND BEEF WITH BASIL, CHILI, AND FRIED EGG

SERVES: 2

Prep Time: 20 minutes (plus 1 hour for infusing the sauce) **Cook Time:** 10 minutes

HOT & SOUR SAUCE

⅓ cup (80 ml) fish sauce
Juice of 2 limes
2–4 bird's eye chilies, thinly sliced (or to taste)
1 clove garlic, minced
1 teaspoon peeled and grated fresh ginger
1 teaspoon honey, *optional*
Fresh cilantro, chopped

GROUND BEEF STIR-FRY

3 tablespoons coconut oil, duck fat, tallow or other good-quality fat, *divided* (plus extra as needed)
2 organic, free-range eggs
2 fresh red chilies, sliced
3 cloves garlic, minced
10½ ounces (300 g) grass-fed ground beef
½ cup (120 ml) Chicken Bone Broth (page 239)
1 teaspoon fish sauce, or to taste
1 teaspoon tamari or coconut aminos, *optional*
1 teaspoon honey, *optional*
¼ teaspoon Chinese five-spice powder
2 large handfuls fresh Thai basil leaves

1. To make the Hot and Sour Sauce: Combine the fish sauce, lime juice, bird's eye chilies, garlic, ginger, and honey (if using) in a small bowl, then mix well and set aside. For best results, make the sauce at least 1 hour, and up to 1 day, in advance—the longer you leave it, the stronger and more intense the flavors of the sauce will be.

2. To make the stir-fry, heat a wok or a large skillet over medium-high heat. Add 1 tablespoon of the coconut oil and swirl it around the pan. Crack one egg into the center and fry until cooked to your liking (1–2 minutes). Shake the wok gently to prevent the egg from sticking. Carefully lift out the egg with a spatula and transfer to a plate to keep warm. Repeat with the other egg, adding a little more oil if needed.

3. Return the wok to high heat. Add the remaining 2 tablespoons of coconut oil and swirl it around the wok. Add the chilies and garlic and cook until fragrant (1 minute). Add the ground beef and stir-fry until brown (2 minutes), then add the chicken broth and simmer for 3 minutes. Mix in the fish sauce, tamari, honey, and five-spice powder. Toss in the basil, and once it has wilted, remove the wok from the heat. Season to taste with sea salt and freshly cracked black pepper.

4. To serve, divide the meat between two serving plates and top each portion with a warm fried egg. Drizzle the hot and sour sauce over the top, then sprinkle with freshly chopped cilantro, serving extra sauce on the side.

HEMP SEED PORRIDGE WITH BLUEBERRY COMPOTE

SERVES: 2

Prep Time: 10 minutes **Cook Time:** 12 minutes

BLUEBERRY COMPOTE

1⅓ cups (200 g) blueberries (fresh or frozen)
1 tablespoon manuka honey or sweetener of your choice (liquid stevia, xylitol, or monk fruit sweetener), to taste

1 cup (150 g) hemp seeds
2 cups (480 ml) coconut or plant-based milk of your choice, plus extra to serve
2 tablespoons shredded coconut
2 tablespoons ground flaxseeds
1 tablespoon chia seeds
1 teaspoon manuka honey or sweetener of your choice (liquid stevia, xylitol, or monk fruit sweetener), to taste
Pinch sea salt
½ teaspoon vanilla powder or paste

1. To make the blueberry compote, place half the blueberries and the honey or sweetener in a small saucepan over low heat. Cook for 5 minutes until the blueberries have slightly broken down. Remove from the heat, stir in the remaining berries, and allow to cool.
2. Combine the hemp seeds, milk of your choice, coconut, flaxseeds, chia seeds, honey or sweetener, and salt in a small saucepan over medium–low heat. Cook, stirring frequently, for 5–7 minutes, or until thickened. Stir in the vanilla.
3. Transfer the porridge to serving bowls, pour over some extra milk, then spoon over the blueberry compote and serve.

TUNA POKE WITH FRIED EGG AND COCONUT TORTILLA

SERVES: 4

Prep Time: 35 minutes **Cook Time:** 16–18 minutes

POKE DRESSING

½ French shallot, finely chopped
1 clove garlic, finely grated
1 scallion, green part thinly sliced and white part finely chopped
½ long red chili, thinly sliced, or ½ teaspoon chili flakes (add more if you like it spicy), *optional*
1 teaspoon finely grated ginger
2 tablespoons tamari or coconut aminos
2 teaspoons sesame oil
2 tablespoons extra-virgin olive oil
1 teaspoon toasted black and white sesame seeds, plus extra to serve

1½ avocados, diced
1½ tablespoons lime juice
1 tablespoon extra-virgin olive oil
Freshly ground black pepper
2 tablespoons coconut oil or good-quality animal fat
4 organic, free-range eggs
1 Persian cucumber, deseeded and cut into matchsticks
1 pound (450 g) sashimi-grade tuna, cut into small cubes
1 lime, cut into wedges
Cilantro leaves, to serve

1. To make the poke dressing, combine all the ingredients in a bowl with 1 tablespoon of water, mix well, and refrigerate for at least 30 minutes to allow the flavors to develop.
2. To make the coconut tortilla, combine the almond meal, tapioca flour, coconut milk, egg, and ½ cup (120 ml) of water in a bowl; mix well and season with salt. Heat a small nonstick skillet over medium heat. Add enough oil to coat the surface of the pan, then pour in 3 tablespoons of batter and swirl around slightly. Cook for 2½ minutes until mostly cooked through, then flip and cook for 1½–2 minutes until golden and crisp. Place the tortilla on a plate and keep warm. Repeat with the remaining mixture to make six tortillas (see TIP below).
3. Slightly crush the avocado with a fork or potato masher and mix in the lime juice and olive oil. Season with salt and pepper.
4. Heat the coconut oil or fat in a skillet over medium heat. Crack in the eggs and cook for 2–3 minutes, or until cooked to your liking. Season with salt and pepper. Keep warm.
5. Place the cucumber in a bowl, pour over 1 tablespoon of poke dressing, and toss to combine. Set aside.
6. Add the tuna to the remaining poke dressing and gently toss. Taste and season with a little salt, if needed.

COCONUT TORTILLA

1 cup (100 g) almond meal
1 cup (125 g) tapioca flour
½ cup (120 ml) coconut milk
1 organic, free-range egg
Sea salt
Coconut oil, for cooking

7. To serve, place a tortilla on each serving plate. Spoon on the avocado mixture, then top with the dressed cucumber and tuna. Squeeze a little lime juice over the tuna as desired, then add a fried egg. Sprinkle on some sesame seeds and serve with the cilantro leaves.

TIP:

Reserve the remaining tortillas for another use. They can be stored in an airtight container in the fridge for up to 1 week or frozen for up to 3 months.

SARDINES ON TOAST

SERVES: 4

Prep Time: 10 minutes **Cook Time:** 15 minutes

- **6 Roma tomatoes, halved**
- **2 tablespoons coconut oil or good-quality animal fat, melted, *divided***
- **Sea salt and freshly ground black pepper**
- **8 slices paleo bread (see Paleo Hemp Bread Loaf recipe page 281)**
- **Garlic-infused olive oil or extra-virgin olive oil, for drizzling**
- **12 whole sardines, cleaned, scaled, and gutted (ask your fishmonger to do this)**

1. Preheat the oven to 400°F (200°C) or 350°F (180°C fan-forced/convection).
2. Heat a barbecue grill plate to hot or a grill pan over high heat.
3. Brush the tomato halves with some of the coconut oil or fat and season with salt and pepper. Grill the tomato halves for 1 minute on each side, or until charred. Transfer to a baking sheet and bake for 8 minutes, or until soft. Place in a bowl and crush with a fork until chunky. Set aside, keeping warm.
4. Next, grill the bread on both sides until crisp, about 1–1½ minutes. Drizzle over the olive oil and set aside.
5. Brush the sardines with the remaining coconut oil or fat and grill for 40 seconds on each side, or until cooked through.
6. To serve, spread the crushed tomato on the grilled bread, then top with the sardines. Season with some extra salt and pepper and drizzle with a little more olive oil.

BEEF SAUSAGES WITH BRAZIL NUT PESTO

SERVES: 2

Prep Time: 15 minutes **Cook Time:** 9 minutes

BRAZIL NUT PESTO

1 large handful sage leaves
2 large handfuls flat-leaf parsley leaves
3–4 cloves garlic
½ cup (80 g) Brazil nuts
2 tablespoons lemon juice
Sea salt and freshly ground black pepper
1 cup (240 ml) extra-virgin olive oil

2 tablespoons coconut oil or good-quality animal fat
6 paleo grass-fed beef sausages (these should be gluten-, grain-, and sugar-free)
Large handful flat-leaf parsley leaves
1 tablespoon extra-virgin olive oil

1. Place all the Brazil nut pesto ingredients in a food processor and whiz to a thick paste. Set aside.
2. Heat the coconut oil or fat in a large skillet over medium heat. Add the sausages and cook on all sides until browned and just cooked through, about 8 minutes.
3. Place the parsley in a small bowl with 1 tablespoon each of olive oil and pesto and toss to coat.
4. Spoon the remaining pesto onto serving plates and top with the sausages and parsley.

HEMP BIRCHER

SERVES: 2

Prep Time: 10–15 minutes (plus overnight to soak)

½ cup (75 g) hemp seeds, plus extra to serve
1 tablespoon chia seeds
2 tablespoons flaxseeds
¼ teaspoon ground cinnamon, plus extra to serve
¼ teaspoon vanilla powder or paste
½ cup (120 g) coconut yogurt, plus extra to serve
¾ cup (175 ml) almond or coconut milk
1 green apple, grated
Sweetener of your choice (such as liquid stevia or honey), to taste, *optional*
Fresh or frozen blueberries, to serve

Note:

You'll need to begin this recipe a day ahead.

1. Place the hemp seeds, chia seeds, flaxseeds, cinnamon, vanilla, coconut yogurt, and almond or coconut milk in a bowl and mix well to combine. Cover and refrigerate overnight.
2. The next morning, mix through the grated apple and sweetener of your choice, if desired, and spoon the bircher into two serving bowls or jars.
3. Top with some extra yogurt, the blueberries, some extra hemp seeds and a little extra cinnamon. Alternatively, layer it up as we've done here.

SPICED PUMPKIN PANCAKES

SERVES: 2–3

Prep Time: 10–15 minutes **Cook Time:** 1 hour (for the pumpkin puree)
10 minutes (for the pancakes)

PUMPKIN PUREE

1½ pounds (700 g) pie pumpkin, peeled and cut into 1¼-inch (3-cm) chunks

5 organic, free-range eggs
⅓ cup (80 ml) nut milk
1 cup (100 g) almond meal
2 tablespoons coconut flour
2 tablespoons maple syrup
2 teaspoons baking powder
1 teaspoon ground cinnamon, plus extra to serve
1 teaspoon ground ginger
¼ teaspoon ground cardamom
Pinch sea salt
Coconut oil, for cooking

TO SERVE

Whipped Coconut Cream (page 282)
Maple syrup
Fresh blueberries

Note:

Store the remaining pumpkin puree in a sealed container in the fridge for up to 10 days.

1. To make the pumpkin puree, preheat the oven to 350°F (180°C) or 325°F (160°C fan-forced / convection).
2. Place the pumpkin in a casserole dish and pour in 3½ tablespoons of water. Cover with a lid and bake for 1 hour, or until very soft and tender. Allow to cool.
3. Place the cooled pumpkin in the bowl of a food processor and process until smooth. (Makes 2⅓ cups/550 g.)
4. Place ⅔ cup (160 g) of the pumpkin puree in a large bowl and add the eggs, nut milk, almond meal, coconut flour, maple syrup, baking powder, cinnamon, ginger, cardamom, and salt. Stir with a whisk to combine.
5. Heat a tablespoon of coconut oil in a large skillet over medium–low heat. Working in batches of three or four, add 3 level tablespoons of batter per pancake and shape into rounds about 4 inches (10 cm) in diameter. Cook the pancakes for 1½ minutes, or until the underside is firm and starts to color. Flip over and cook on the other side for 1 minute, or until lightly golden.
6. Transfer to a warm plate. Repeat, adding more oil as necessary, until all the batter is used.
7. Pile the pancakes onto plates in stacks of three or four and serve with whipped coconut cream, maple syrup, blueberries, and a dusting of cinnamon.

SIMPLE COCONUT YOGURT

YIELD: 1½ QUARTS (1.5 LITERS)

Prep Time: 15 minutes, plus 12 hours fermenting time **Cook Time:** 5 minutes

- **1 tablespoon unflavored powdered gelatin**
- **3 (13½-ounce/400 ml) cans coconut milk**
- **1 vanilla pod, split and seeds scraped, *optional***
- **1–2 tablespoons honey, maple syrup or coconut sugar**
- **3 probiotic capsules or ¼ teaspoon nondairy starter culture**

TIP:

Taste the yogurt after 12 hours. If you prefer a tangier taste, you can leave it to ferment for another couple of hours. If you're using raw honey as your sweetener, use it with caution—raw honey has natural antimicrobial properties that can interfere with the growth of beneficial bacteria during fermentation. To avoid this, either use pasteurized honey or gently heat raw honey before adding it to your coconut milk mixture. This reduces its antimicrobial effect and ensures proper culturing.

1. You'll need a 1½-quart (1.5 liter) preserving jar with a lid for this recipe. Wash the jar and all utensils thoroughly in very hot water or run them through a hot rinse cycle in the dishwasher.
2. Place 3 tablespoons of filtered water in a small bowl, sprinkle on the gelatin, and soak for 2 minutes.
3. Place the coconut milk and vanilla seeds (if using) in a saucepan and gently heat, stirring with a spoon, over medium–low heat until just starting to simmer (195°F / 90°C, if testing with a thermometer). Do not allow to boil. Immediately remove the pan from the heat. While still hot, mix in the gelatine mixture, then add the sweetener and mix well. Cover the pan with a lid and set aside to cool to lukewarm (95°F / 35°C or less).
4. Pour ½ cup (125 ml) of the cooled coconut milk mixture into a sterilized bowl. Open the probiotic capsules (if using). Stir the yogurt starter or probiotic powder into the coconut milk in the bowl. Add the remaining coconut milk and mix well.
5. Pour the coconut milk mixture into the sterilized jar and loosely seal the lid. Ferment in a warm spot for 12 hours at 100–104°F (38–40°C). To maintain this temperature and allow the yogurt to culture, wrap your jar in a tea towel and place it on a plate in the oven with the door shut and the oven light on. The light's warmth will keep the temperature consistent. Alternatively, place the

(Continued . . .)

Note:

For those doing AIP, natural sweetener is allowed in this recipe as it is needed for the fermentation process. The bacteria fermenting the coconut milk consume the sugar, not you.

tea towel–wrapped jar in a cooler, fill a heatproof container with boiling water, and place it beside the jar—do not allow them to touch—and close the lid. Replace the boiling water halfway through the fermenting process.

6. Once fermented, the yogurt tends to form air bubbles and looks as though it has separated. Stir well and refrigerate for at least 5 hours before eating. If it separates after chilling, give it a good whisk. Store in the fridge for up to 2 weeks.

MAHA MEAT: SAVOR THE MOMENT, ANY TIME

Welcome to the heart of MAHA's kitchen, where meat takes center stage with bold, soul-warming flavors. Imagine a table brimming with juicy grilled skewers, tender slowly cooked meats, or a delicious roast that melts in your mouth. This chapter is all about celebrating the joy of meat, cooked with care and shared with love. At MAHA, these recipes embrace grass-fed and wild-sourced meats not only for delicious flavor but also for ethical reasons, and supporting the farmers who buck the system, while keeping things budget friendly with ground cuts and offal. Whether you're firing up the grill or simmering a cozy stew, it's about creating dishes that bring people together, no matter the hour. From farmers' markets and wonderful butchers to your plate, these recipes invite you to cook with passion and savor every bite. So, grab a seat, turn up your favorite playlist, and let's make something deliciously unforgettable, any time you please.

SUPER SIMPLE BURGERS

SERVES: 4

Prep Time: 20 minutes **Cook Time:** 12–15 minutes

PATTIES

- 1½ pounds (680 g) grass-fed ground beef
- 1 onion, finely diced
- 2 cloves garlic, finely chopped
- 2 tablespoons chopped flat-leaf parsley leaves
- 1 teaspoon dried oregano
- 2 tablespoons coconut aminos or tamari
- 1½ teaspoons sea salt
- 1 teaspoon freshly ground black pepper

- 4 tablespoons coconut oil or good-quality animal fat, *divided*
- 1 large onion, sliced
- 2 tomatoes, thinly sliced
- 8 baby cos (romaine) lettuce leaves
- Tomato ketchup (to make your own, see page 246 or use store-bought, sugar-free and gluten-free), to serve

1. To make the patties, place all the ingredients in a large bowl and mix well using your hands until well combined.
2. Divide the mixture into 8 equal portions and shape into patties about ½ inch (1.25 cm) thick.
3. Heat 2 tablespoons of the coconut oil or fat in a large skillet over medium heat. Add the sliced onion and cook for 8–10 minutes, stirring occasionally, until softened and golden. Remove from the pan and set aside.
4. Heat the remaining 2 tablespoons of coconut oil or fat in the same pan over medium-high heat. Cook the patties for 3–4 minutes on each side, or until nicely browned and cooked through. If cooking in batches, keep the first batch warm while you finish the rest.
5. To serve, layer each patty between two baby cos lettuce leaves, along with tomato slices, cooked onion, and a spoonful of tomato ketchup.

CRISPY PORK SLIDERS WITH KIMCHI, PICKLED CUCUMBER & SRIRACHA MAYO

SERVES: 4

Prep Time: 30 minutes **Cook Time:** 2 hours (plus 15 minutes resting time)

CRISPY PORK

2½ pounds (1.1 kg) boneless pork belly, skin scored, at room temperature
1 cup (250 ml) boiling water
2 tablespoons coconut oil or good-quality animal fat
Sea salt

PICKLED CUCUMBER

1 Persian cucumber, thinly sliced
2 tablespoons apple cider vinegar
½ teaspoon sea salt
1 teaspoon maple syrup or honey

TO ASSEMBLE

8 mini charcoal slider buns or small paleo rolls, halved (page 279)
¾ cup (180 g) kimchi (page 266)
8 iceberg lettuce leaves, torn
Sriracha Mayo (page 245)

TO MAKE THE CRISPY PORK:

1. Preheat the oven to 460°F (240°C) or 430°F (220°C convection/fan-forced). Place the pork belly on a wire rack set over the kitchen sink. Carefully pour the boiling water over the skin to help open up the surface. Pat the pork completely dry with paper towels.
2. Rub the coconut oil or fat into the skin, then season generously with sea salt.
3. Place the pork in a large, deep roasting pan and roast for 35–40 minutes, or until the skin starts to bubble and blister.
4. Reduce the oven temperature to 300°F (150°C) or 265°F (130°C convection/fan-forced). Continue roasting the pork for 1¼ hours, or until the meat is very tender.
5. Remove the pork from the oven and let it rest for 15 minutes, keeping it loosely covered to stay warm.
6. If the crackling isn't crisp enough, place the pork, crackling-side up, under a hot broiler (grill) for a few minutes until it crisps up.
7. Slice the pork into small pieces suitable for sliders.

TO MAKE THE PICKLED CUCUMBER:

In a small bowl, combine the cucumber slices, apple cider vinegar, salt, and maple syrup. Toss to coat and let sit for at least 15 minutes to quick pickle.

TO ASSEMBLE THE SLIDERS:

1. Lightly toast the buns or rolls, if desired.
2. Spread sriracha mayo on the bottom halves, then layer with iceberg lettuce, crispy pork, pickled cucumber, kimchi, and iceberg lettuce.
3. Add the top halves of the buns, press gently, and serve immediately.

SPAGHETTI BOLOGNESE

SERVES: 4

Prep Time: 20 minutes **Cook Time:** 45 minutes

SPAGHETTI

3 zucchini
2 carrots

2 tablespoons coconut oil or good-quality animal fat
1 yellow onion, chopped
1 carrot, diced
1 celery stalk, finely diced
4 cloves garlic, finely chopped
1¼ pounds (550 g) grass-fed ground beef (or ground venison, kangaroo, lamb, or emu)
2 tablespoons tomato paste
1 tablespoon chopped oregano leaves
¾ cup (180 ml) dry, preservative-free red wine
2 cups (480 g) tomato puree or whole peeled tomatoes, crushed
1¼ cups (300 ml) Chicken Bone Broth (page 239)
Pinch red pepper flakes, *optional*
Sea salt and freshly ground black pepper
Baby basil leaves, to serve

1. To make the spaghetti, use the thick noodle blade on a spiralizer to create carrot and zucchini noodles. If you don't have a spiralizer, simply julienne the carrot and zucchini using a sharp knife. Set aside until needed.
2. Melt the oil or fat in a large skillet over medium–high heat. Add the onion, carrot, and celery and cook for 4–5 minutes until the onion is soft. Stir in the garlic and cook for 1 minute until fragrant and starting to brown. Add the ground beef and brown, breaking up any lumps with a wooden spoon, for 5–6 minutes. Add the tomato paste, stir and cook for 1 minute. Mix in the oregano and wine and cook for 4–5 minutes until the wine has almost evaporated. Add the tomato puree, half the broth, and the red pepper flakes (if using) and season with salt and pepper.
3. Simmer on low heat for 30 minutes, adding more broth if needed.
4. Bring a saucepan of salted water to boil. Add the carrot noodles and cook for 30 seconds, then add the zucchini noodles and cook for a further 30 seconds until just tender. Drain well.
5. Spoon the noodles into four serving bowls, top with the Bolognese, then sprinkle on the basil.

CHILI CON CARNE

SERVES: 4–6

Prep Time: 20 minutes **Cook Time:** 45 minutes

- 2 tablespoons coconut oil or good-quality animal fat
- 1 yellow onion, finely chopped
- 1 large carrot, chopped
- ½ red bell pepper, deseeded and chopped
- 3 cloves garlic, finely chopped
- 1–2 long red chilis, deseeded and finely chopped
- 1⅓ pounds (600 g) grass-fed ground beef
- 2 teaspoons smoked paprika
- 2 teaspoons ground cumin
- 1 teaspoon ground coriander
- ¼ teaspoon chili powder (add another ¼ teaspoon if you like it extra spicy)
- 2½ teaspoons dried oregano
- 2½ tablespoons tomato paste
- 1¾ cups (400 g) diced tomatoes
- 1 cup (240 ml) Beef Bone Broth (page 238), plus extra if needed
- Sea salt and freshly ground black pepper

1. Heat the coconut oil or animal fat in a large skillet over medium heat. Add the onion, carrot, and bell pepper and cook for 8 minutes, or until softened. Stir in the garlic and chilis and cook for 1 minute, or until fragrant.
2. Add the ground beef to the pan and cook, stirring with a wooden spoon to break up the lumps, for 5 minutes, or until browned. Add the spices, oregano, and tomato paste and cook for 1 minute, then mix in the tomatoes and broth.
3. Reduce the heat to low and simmer for 30 minutes, adding more broth if needed. Season with salt and a good grind of pepper and serve.

GROUND BEEF CURRY

SERVES: 4–6

Prep Time: 30 minutes **Cook Time:** 30 minutes

2 tablespoons coconut oil
1 large onion, finely chopped
2 carrots, diced
2 tomatoes, chopped
1 red chili, deseeded and finely chopped
1 teaspoon black or brown mustard seeds
10 fresh curry leaves
4 cloves garlic, finely chopped
1½ tablespoons garam masala
2 teaspoons ground coriander
2 teaspoons ground cumin
½ teaspoon ground cardamom
½ teaspoon ground ginger
2 teaspoons ground turmeric
2 pinches of cayenne pepper, *optional*
1½ pounds (700 g) grass-fed ground beef
1 turnip, diced
1 (13-ounce/400-ml) can coconut cream
1 cup (250 ml) Beef or Chicken Bone Broth (see recipes on pages 238 and 239)
Juice of 1 lemon
Sea salt and freshly ground black pepper

TO SERVE

Cilantro leaves
Lime wedges
Cauliflower Rice (page 286)

1. Melt the oil in a wok or large skillet over medium heat. Add the onion, carrot, and tomato and cook, stirring occasionally, for 8 minutes until the vegetables are soft.
2. Add the chili pepper to the pan and cook for 1 minute, then add the mustard seeds and cook for 15–20 seconds until they begin to pop. Stir in the curry leaves and garlic and sauté for 10 seconds, then add the dried spices and cook, stirring frequently, for 30 seconds until fragrant. Add the ground beef and cook, breaking up any lumps with a wooden spoon, for 5 minutes until browned. Stir in the turnip, coconut cream, and broth and bring to a boil.
3. Reduce the heat to low and simmer for 20 minutes until the sauce is slightly thickened and the beef and vegetables are cooked through.
4. Mix in the lemon juice and season with salt and pepper. Scatter on the cilantro leaves and serve with lime wedges and cauliflower rice.

CHILI BEEF FAJITA WITH SWEET POTATO WEDGES

SERVES: 4

Prep Time: 15 minutes (plus 15 minutes marinating time) **Cook Time:** 70 minutes

- 3 sweet potatoes (about 1¾ lb/800 g), cut into 1-inch (2.5-cm) wedges
- ⅓ cup (100 ml) melted coconut oil or good-quality animal fat, *divided*
- Sea salt and freshly ground black pepper
- 1½ pounds (700 g) grass-fed beef sirloin or tri-tip, fat and sinew removed, cut into strips
- Juice of ½ lime, plus extra to serve
- ½ teaspoon ground cumin
- 1 teaspoon smoked paprika
- 2 teaspoons chipotle chilies in adobo sauce
- 1 yellow onion, sliced
- 1 red bell pepper, deseeded and sliced
- 4 cloves garlic, finely chopped
- 14 ounces (400 g) diced tomatoes (canned or jarred)
- 1 handful cilantro sprigs
- Lime wedges, to serve

1. Preheat the oven to 400°F (200°C) or 350°F (180°C fan-forced/convection). Lightly grease a large baking sheet.
2. Place the sweet potato wedges in a bowl, add 2 tablespoons of the coconut oil or fat, season with salt and pepper, and mix well. Spread the wedges out on the prepared baking sheet in a single layer. Roast for about 20 minutes, then turn the wedges over and roast for another 20 minutes, or until tender and golden.
3. Meanwhile, place the beef strips, lime juice, spices, and chipotle chilis in adobo sauce in a nonreactive bowl and season with salt and pepper. Toss the meat to coat. Cover and marinate at room temperature for 15 minutes.
4. Heat 2 tablespoons of the oil or fat in a heavy-based skillet over medium–high heat. Add the onion and sauté for 3 minutes, or until softened. Add the bell pepper and sauté for 5 minutes, or until slightly softened. Stir in the garlic and sauté for 30 seconds, or until fragrant. Pour in the tomatoes and ½ cup (120 ml) of water. Reduce the heat to medium–low and simmer for 15 minutes. Season to taste with salt and pepper.
5. Heat the remaining oil or fat in a large, heavy-based skillet over medium–high heat. Add the marinated beef strips in batches, and sauté for 2 minutes until slightly charred and medium–rare, or cook to your liking. Add the vegetable mixture and mix to combine.
6. Scatter the cilantro sprigs over the chili beef and serve with the sweet potato and lime wedges.

BACON-WRAPPED OFFAL MUFFINS WITH PICKLE SALAD & MUSTARD MAYO

SERVES: 4
MAKES: 8 MUFFINS

Prep Time: 30 minutes **Cook Time:** 30 minutes

MUFFINS

5⅓ ounces (150 g) organic, free-range chicken livers
5⅓ ounces (150 g) grass-fed beef heart
2 ounces (60 g) grass-fed bone marrow flesh (ask your butcher)
14 ounces (400 g) grass-fed ground beef
½ onion, finely diced
2 cloves garlic, finely chopped
2 organic, free-range eggs
1½ tablespoons chopped flat-leaf parsley
½ teaspoon dried oregano
1 teaspoon sea salt
½ teaspoon freshly ground black pepper
12 slices streaky bacon

PICKLE SALAD

½ cup (80 g) pickled onions (page 270)
2 small dill pickles or gherkins, sliced lengthwise
4 artichoke hearts (canned or jarred), halved
4 radishes, thinly sliced
1 cup (30 g) baby arugula (rocket)
2 tablespoon extra-virgin olive oil
1 teaspoon apple cider vinegar
Sea salt and freshly ground black pepper, to taste

1. Preheat the oven to 350°F (180°C). Lightly grease a 12-cup muffin tray or line with strips of baking paper.
2. Rinse, pat dry, and trim the chicken livers and beef heart, removing any sinew and veins. Dice the beef heart.
3. Add the liver, heart, and marrow to a food processor and pulse until finely ground.
4. Transfer to a large bowl with the ground beef, onion, garlic, eggs, parsley, oregano, salt, and pepper. Mix until well combined.
5. Line each muffin cup with 1 slice of bacon, wrapping it around the sides. Fill each with the meat mixture and press down lightly.
6. Bake for 25–30 minutes, or until cooked through and browned on top. Let cool slightly before removing from the tray.

TO MAKE THE PICKLE SALAD

1. In a bowl, combine the pickled onion, sliced pickles, artichoke hearts, radishes, and arugula.
2. Drizzle with olive oil and apple cider vinegar, then season with salt and pepper. Toss gently to combine.

MUSTARD MAYO

½ cup (120 ml) mayonnaise (page 244 or store-bought)
1 tablespoon Dijon mustard
1 teaspoon lemon juice

TO MAKE THE MUSTARD MAYO

1. Stir together mayonnaise, Dijon mustard, and lemon juice until smooth. Refrigerate until ready to serve.

TO SERVE

Plate two muffins with a generous serving of pickle salad and a spoonful of mustard mayo. Finish with cracked black pepper and a few fresh arugula leaves, if desired.

THAI PORK SKEWERS WITH LETTUCE CUPS & NAM JIM

SERVES: 4
MAKES: 10–12 SKEWERS

Prep Time: 30 minutes (plus 30 minutes marinating) **Cook Time:** 12–15 minutes

FOR THE SKEWERS

2 cloves garlic, chopped
1 shallot, chopped
¼ bunch cilantro (coriander), stems and leaves, chopped
1 lemongrass stalk (white part only), chopped
1 tablespoon fish sauce
1 tablespoon tamari or coconut aminos
1 tablespoon coconut sugar or raw honey
1 tablespoon coconut cream
1 teaspoon lime zest
½ teaspoon sea salt
½ teaspoon ground white pepper
1 pound (450 g) ground (minced) pork
10–12 lemongrass stalks or skewers

TO SERVE

Lettuce cups (iceberg or butter lettuce)
Fresh herbs: mint, Thai basil, cilantro
Cucumber ribbons or shaved cucumber
Paleo Nam Jim (page 249)
Lime wedges
Sliced red chili, *optional*
Sesame seeds, for garnish, *optional*

1. In a food processor, add the garlic, shallot, cilantro (stems and leaves), and lemongrass. Blend until finely chopped. Add the fish sauce, tamari, coconut sugar or honey, coconut cream, lime zest, salt, and pepper. Blend again until well combined.
2. Transfer the mixture to a mixing bowl. Add the ground pork and mix thoroughly until evenly combined.
3. Cover and refrigerate for at least 30 minutes, or up to 12 hours.
4. Divide the mixture into 10–12 portions. Mold each portion around the end of a lemongrass stalk or skewer, shaping into elongated sausages.
5. To grill: Preheat a outdoor grill over medium-high heat. Drizzle the pork skewers with oil and grill the skewers for 6–7 minutes, turning frequently, until golden brown and cooked through. OR
To bake: Preheat the oven to 400°F (200°C). Line a tray with parchment paper and bake for 12–15 minutes, turning halfway through, until cooked through and slightly caramelized.

TO SERVE:

Arrange the skewers on a serving platter. Serve with lettuce cups, fresh herbs, cucumber ribbons, lime wedges, and Paleo Nam Jim (see recipe). Garnish with red chili slices and sesame seeds, if desired.

PULLED PORK BURGER

SERVES: 4

Prep Time: 15 minutes **Cook Time:** 2–3 minutes to warm the meat

COLESLAW

1 small carrot, grated
¼ small red onion, thinly sliced
¼ small red cabbage, finely shredded
1 tablespoon lemon juice
⅓ cup (80 ml) Aioli (page 245) or Mayonnaise (page 244)
Sea salt and freshly ground black pepper, to taste
1 handful flat-leaf parsley, roughly chopped

½ quantity Pulled Pork (page 96)
4 paleo burger buns (page 279)
4 tablespoons smoky BBQ sauce (page 248 or store-bought, gluten-free and sugar-free)
4 tablespoons chipotle aioli (page 246)
Sweet potato wedges, to serve (page 77)

1. **To make the coleslaw:** In a large bowl, combine the grated carrot, sliced onion, and shredded cabbage. Set aside.
2. In a small bowl, whisk together the lemon juice and aioli or mayonnaise until smooth to make the dressing.
3. When ready to serve, season the vegetables with salt and pepper, add the parsley, and pour in the dressing. Toss well to coat evenly.
4. **Assemble the burgers:** Warm the pulled pork if needed. Slice the paleo buns in half. On the bottom half of each bun, layer a generous spoonful of coleslaw, followed by pulled pork, a dollop of BBQ sauce, and chipotle mayo. Top with the bun lids and serve with sweet potato wedges on the side.

HOT DOGS

SERVES: 4

Prep Time: 10 minutes **Cook Time:** 10–12 minutes

- **2 tablespoons coconut oil or good-quality animal fat, plus extra if needed**
- **1 large yellow onion, sliced**
- **Sea salt and freshly ground black pepper**
- **4 paleo beef hot dogs (gluten-free, grain-free and dairy-free)**
- **4 baby romaine lettuce leaves**
- **⅓ cup (50 g) sliced dill pickles**
- **⅓ cup (80 g) tomato ketchup (to make your own go to page 246 or store-bought sugar-free and gluten-free)**
- **Brown or Dijon mustard, to serve**

1. Melt the coconut oil or fat in a nonstick skillet over medium heat. Add the onion and sauté for 6 minutes, or until softened and starting to caramelize. Season with salt and pepper, then remove from the pan and set aside, keeping warm.
2. Heat an outdoor grill plate to medium–hot or a grill pan over medium–high heat. Brush with some extra coconut oil or fat if needed, then add the hot dogs and cook for 6–8 minutes until heated through and charred. Set aside, keeping warm. Alternatively, fill a saucepan with water and bring to a gentle simmer (do not boil). Add the hot dogs and cook for 5 minutes, or until heated through. Carefully remove the hot dogs with a slotted spoon or tongs and place on paper towel to drain.
3. Place a hot dog lengthways in the center of a lettuce leaf. Scatter over the onion and pickle, then dollop on some ketchup and mustard and serve.

MINI MEATY MUFFINS

SERVES: 6

Prep Time: 15 minutes **Cook Time:** 24 minutes

- **1 tablespoon coconut oil or other good-quality fat**
- **2 cloves garlic, finely chopped**
- **1 yellow onion, finely chopped**
- **1 handful kale leaves, finely chopped**
- **1 small carrot, grated**
- **1 tablespoon tomato paste**
- **½ cup (120 ml) barbecue sauce (to make your own, see page 248 or use store-bought, sugar-free and gluten-free)**
- **1 tablespoon Worcestershire sauce**
- **½ teaspoon ground cumin**
- **1 pound (450 g) grass-fed ground beef or lamb**
- **7 ounces (200 g) minced free-range chicken, lamb, or grass-fed beef liver**
- **1 organic, free-range egg**
- **½ cup (50 g) fresh paleo breadcrumbs**
- **½ teaspoon dried oregano**
- **1 teaspoon finely chopped parsley**
- **½ teaspoon salt**

1. Preheat the oven to 350°F (180°C). Lightly grease a 24-cup mini muffin tray with coconut oil.
2. Heat the oil in a skillet over medium heat. Add the garlic and onion, and sauté for about 3 minutes, until translucent and beginning to color. Add the kale and carrot and cook for another 2 minutes to soften. Remove from the heat and set aside.
3. In a small bowl, mix together the tomato paste, barbecue sauce, Worcestershire sauce, and cumin to make the sauce.
4. In a large bowl, combine the ground meat, minced liver, egg, breadcrumbs, oregano, parsley, salt and half of the sauce. Add the vegetable mixture and mix everything until well combined.
5. Spoon the mixture evenly into the prepared muffin cups.
6. Bake in the oven for 15 minutes or until cooked through.
7. Meanwhile, heat the remaining sauce over medium low until warmed through.
8. Serve the meaty muffins with the sauce and some salad on the side.

Notes:

- Ask your butcher to mince the liver for you or process it in a blender or food processor at home.
- These muffins are also great for batch cooking and freezing.

ITALIAN-STYLE MEATBALLS WITH ZUCCHINI ZOODLES

SERVES: 4

Prep Time: 30 minutes (plus 30 minutes chilling) **Cook Time:** 50 minutes

TOMATO AND BASIL SAUCE

1 tablespoon coconut oil or good-quality animal fat
1 yellow onion, chopped
4 cloves garlic, crushed
2 tablespoons tomato paste
14 ounces (400 g) whole peeled tomatoes, crushed (see Note on page 105)
1⅔ cups (400 ml) Chicken Bone Broth (page 239) or water
1 teaspoon dried oregano

MEATBALLS

3 tablespoons coconut oil or good-quality animal fat, *divided*
½ yellow onion, finely chopped
3 cloves garlic, finely chopped
1 teaspoon fennel seeds, crushed
1 pound (450 g) ground pork
7 ounces (200 g) ground beef
3 tablespoons chopped flat-leaf parsley leaves
1 organic, free-range egg
2 tablespoons almond meal
¼ teaspoon chili flakes, *optional*
Sea salt and freshly ground black pepper

1. **To make the tomato and basil sauce:** Heat the coconut oil or fat in a saucepan over medium heat. Add the onion and cook for 5 minutes, or until softened. Add the garlic and tomato paste and sauté for 1 minute, or until fragrant.
2. Add the crushed tomatoes, broth or water, oregano, and basil. Bring to a simmer. Reduce heat to medium–low and cook for 30 minutes, or until the sauce is rich in flavor. Season with salt and pepper. Blend with an immersion blender until smooth, then stir in the olive oil. Set aside.
3. **To make the meatballs:** Heat half the coconut oil or fat in a large skillet over medium heat. Add the onion and cook for 5 minutes, or until translucent. Stir in the garlic and fennel seeds and cook for 1 minute, or until the garlic starts to color. Remove from heat and allow to cool slightly.
4. In a large bowl, combine the ground pork, beef, cooked onion mixture, parsley, egg, almond meal, chili flakes (if using), and a pinch of salt and pepper. Mix until well incorporated. Refrigerate for 30 minutes to firm up the mixture.
5. Roll the mixture into walnut-sized balls. Heat the remaining coconut oil or fat in a large skillet over medium–high heat. Fry the meatballs in batches, if necessary, for about 3 minutes, or until golden on all sides.

6 basil leaves, torn, plus extra to serve
Sea salt and freshly ground black pepper
2 tablespoons extra-virgin olive oil

ZUCCHINI ZOODLES

1 tablespoon olive oil or coconut oil
4 medium zucchini, spiralized (about 6 cups/600 g)
Sea salt and freshly ground black pepper, to taste

6. Pour in the tomato and basil sauce, bring to a simmer, then reduce heat to medium–low. Cover and cook for 15–18 minutes, or until the meatballs are fully cooked through.
7. **To prepare the zucchini zoodles:** Heat the olive oil in a large skillet over medium heat. Add the spiralized zucchini and sauté for 2–3 minutes, tossing gently, until just tender but not mushy. Season with salt and pepper to taste.
8. Divide the zoodles among plates. Top with meatballs and plenty of sauce. Garnish with extra basil leaves and a grind of black pepper.

SAUSAGE AND VEGETABLE SOUP

SERVES:6

Prep Time: 15 minutes **Cook Time:** 50 minutes

1 tablespoon coconut oil or good-quality animal fat
6 grass-fed paleo beef sausages
2 yellow onions, chopped
2 slices free-range bacon, chopped
3 cloves garlic, sliced
2 celery stalks, sliced
2 carrots, cut into ½-inch (1-cm) cubes
1 turnip, cut into ½-inch (1-cm) cubes
3 quarts (3 liters) Beef or Chicken Bone Broth (recipes on pages 238 and 239)
½ teaspoon ground turmeric
½ teaspoon ground cumin
2 zucchini, cut into ½-inch (1-cm) cubes
10½ ounces (300 g) kabocha squash, cut into ¾-inch (2-cm) pieces
2 large handfuls of Swiss chard leaves, stalks removed, roughly chopped
Sea salt and freshly ground black pepper
Juice of 1 lemon

1. Heat the oil or fat in a large saucepan over medium–high heat. Add the sausages and cook for 8 minutes, turning occasionally to brown all over and cooked through.
2. Remove from the pan and, when cool enough to handle, cut into ¾-inch (2-cm) pieces.
3. Reduce the heat to medium, add the onion and bacon to the pan and cook, stirring often, for 5 minutes until soft. Add the garlic, celery, carrots, and turnip. Pour in the broth, stir in the turmeric and cumin, and bring to a boil.
4. Reduce the heat to medium–low, cover, and simmer for 15 minutes.
5. Add the zucchini and squash to the pan and cook for a further 15 minutes, or until the zucchini and squash are soft.
6. Stir in the Swiss chard and sausages and continue to cook for 5 minutes or until heated through.
7. Season with salt and pepper and stir through the lemon juice. Ladle the soup into warmed bowls and serve.

MEATZZA

SERVES: 2–3

Prep Time: 15–20 minutes **Cook Time:** 15–18 minutes

BASE

7 ounces (200 g) ground beef
7 ounces (200 g) ground pork
1 organic, free-range egg yolk
¼ yellow onion, finely diced
1 clove garlic, finely chopped
1 tablespoon finely chopped flat-leaf parsley leaves
½ teaspoon dried oregano
¾ teaspoon sea salt
¼ teaspoon freshly ground black pepper

Coconut oil, for greasing
⅓ cup (80 ml) Pizza Sauce (page 259)
6 basil leaves, roughly torn, plus extra leaves to serve
1 Roma tomato, finely sliced
¾ cup (80 g) vegan mozzarella, torn into small pieces
Sea salt and freshly ground black pepper

1. Preheat the oven to 480°F (250°C) or 445°F (230°C fan-forced/convection) or the highest temperature setting. Grease a 12-inch (30-cm) pizza tray with a little coconut oil and line with parchment paper.
2. Place all the base ingredients in a bowl and mix until well combined.
3. Transfer the base mixture to the prepared tray and, using your hands, press it out to evenly cover the surface. Bake for 6–8 minutes until the meat is cooked through. Remove and drain any liquid from the tray.
4. Spread the pizza sauce evenly over the base. Scatter over the torn basil leaves, then arrange the tomato slices and vegan mozzarella on top. Season with a little salt and pepper.
5. Return the meatzza to the oven and bake for a further 5–10 minutes until lightly browned.
6. Use the paper to carefully transfer the meatzza to a chopping board or plate. Cut into slices, scatter over the extra basil leaves, and serve.

ROAST PORK WITH CABBAGE AND GREMOLATA

SERVES: 8

Prep Time: 10 minutes **Cook Time:** 1 hour 40 min

- **4½ pounds (2 kg) rolled pork loin, skin scored, tied at 2-inch (5-cm) intervals with kitchen string, at room temperature**
- **½ (about 1⅓ pounds / 600 g) savoy cabbage, cut into 1¼-inch (3-cm) slices**
- **2 cups (480 ml) plain kombucha**
- **Sea salt and freshly ground black pepper**
- **2 tablespoons coconut oil or good-quality animal fat**
- **2 teaspoons Pork Seasoning (page 264)**
- **⅔ cup (160 g) Pistachio Gremolata (page 287)**

1. Preheat the oven to 400°F (200°C) or 350°F (180°C fan-forced/convection).
2. Season the pork generously with salt and pepper.
3. Heat the coconut oil or fat in a large oven-safe Dutch oven or flameproof casserole dish over medium heat, add the pork and cook, turning occasionally, for 5–10 minutes until the skin begins to brown. Turn the pork, skin-side up, in the dish. Scatter the cabbage around the pork, pour in the kombucha, and bring to a boil. Remove from the heat, sprinkle over the pork seasoning, then cover with the lid and roast in the oven for 1½ hours.
4. Place the pork, skin-side up, in a large roasting pan and place under a hot broiler for a few minutes to crisp up the crackling. Keep a close eye on the pork at all times, as the crackling can burn very quickly. Transfer to a plate and allow to rest for 5 minutes, keeping warm.
5. Thickly slice the pork and serve with the cabbage and some gremolata spooned over the top.

PULLED PORK LETTUCE TACOS

SERVES: 6

Prep Time: 25–30 minutes (plus 2 hours, or overnight to marinate)
Cook Time: 4 hours and 10 minutes

PASTE

- 6 cloves garlic, peeled
- 1 tablespoon cilantro roots, roughly chopped
- 1 yellow onion, roughly chopped
- 1 jalapeño pepper, deseeded
- 3 tablespoons apple cider vinegar
- 3 tablespoons lard or other good-quality animal fat
- 2 tablespoons chipotle peppers in adobo sauce
- 3 tablespoons tomato paste
- 1 tablespoon smoked paprika
- 1 tablespoon ground cumin

- 4 pounds (1.8 kg) free-range boneless pork shoulder, skin and half the fat removed (save the fat for rendering, see page 277, and the skin for crackling), at room temperature
- Sea salt and freshly ground black pepper
- 3 fresh bay leaves
- 2 cups (480 ml) Beef or Chicken Bone Broth (page 238 or 239)

GUACAMOLE

- 3 avocados, mashed with a fork
- 1 teaspoon ground coriander
- 1 teaspoon ground cumin
- Juice of 1–2 limes
- 1 tablespoon olive oil

1. Place all the paste ingredients in a food processor and blitz until a wet but slightly chunky paste forms.
2. Season the pork with salt and pepper and place in a large Dutch oven or ovenproof casserole dish. Spread the paste over the pork and press the bay leaves on top. Cover and marinate in the fridge for 2 hours or, for best results, overnight.
3. When you're ready to cook, preheat the oven to 285°F (140°C).
4. Pour the beef or chicken broth around the pork into the dish, cover with the lid, and braise for 4 hours, or until the pork is tender. Remove the pork from the liquid and set aside, keeping warm. Place the casserole dish with the liquid over medium–high heat and cook for about 10 minutes, stirring occasionally, until the liquid has reduced by half. Meanwhile, shred the pork. When the liquid has reduced by half, add the shredded pork back to the pot and stir for 3 minutes to heat through. Season with a little more salt and pepper if needed.
5. Place all the guacamole ingredients in a bowl, season with salt to taste, and mix to combine.
6. Spoon the pulled pork into serving bowls and serve with romaine lettuce leaves, pickled red onion, cabbage, cilantro sprigs, guacamole, and lime wedges.

TO SERVE

Baby romaine lettuce leaves
Pickled Red Onion (page 270)
Shredded cabbage leaves
Cilantro sprigs
Lime wedges

TIP:

Any leftover pulled pork can be stored in the freezer for up to 3 months.

CURRIED BEEF PIES WITH PARSNIP MASH

SERVES: 6

Prep Time: 30–40 minutes **Cook Time:** 5 hours

3 tablespoons coconut oil or good-quality animal fat
2¼ pounds (1 kg) grass-fed beef cheek, trimmed and cut into 1-inch (2.5-cm) cubes
1½ onions, finely chopped
1 carrot, finely chopped
1 celery stalk, finely chopped
3 cloves garlic, finely chopped
7 ounces (200 g) grass-fed ground beef
2 tablespoons curry powder
2½ cups (600 ml) Beef Bone Broth (page 238)
14½ ounces (400 g) whole peeled tomatoes, crushed
2 tablespoons tapioca flour, mixed with 2 tablespoons water
Sea salt and freshly ground black pepper
2 teaspoons lemon juice
1 teaspoon yellow mustard seeds
1 teaspoon brown mustard seeds
2 tablespoons olive oil
2 sprigs Crispy Curry Leaves (page 278)

PARSNIP MASH

½ garlic bulb, kept intact (break a whole bulb in half with your hands)
2 tablespoons olive oil, plus extra for drizzling
2 large parsnips (about 1 pound / 450 g), peeled and core removed, chopped

1. Heat 2 tablespoons of the coconut oil or animal fat in a large flameproof casserole dish over medium–high heat. Add the beef cubes in batches and cook for 5 minutes, or until browned on all sides. Transfer the meat to a plate and set aside.
2. Add the remaining oil or fat to the dish, add the onion, carrot, celery, and garlic and sauté for 5 minutes until the onion is softened. Reduce the heat to medium, add the ground beef, and, stirring with a wooden spoon to break up the lumps, cook for 3 minutes, or until browned. Stir in the curry powder and cook for a further minute, or until fragrant. Pour in the broth and tomatoes, then return the beef cubes, stir, and bring to a simmer. Cover with the lid, reduce the heat to low, and simmer for 3 hours, or until the meat is tender.
3. Stir the tapioca mixture into the beef and simmer, uncovered, for 30 minutes, or until the sauce is thickened. Season with salt and pepper and allow to cool. Stir in the lemon juice.
4. Preheat the oven to 350°F (175°C).
5. Place the yellow and brown mustard seeds in a skillet over medium heat and cook, tossing frequently, until fragrant and toasted. Pour on the olive oil; remove from the heat and set aside.
6. To start on the parsnip mash, place the garlic on a baking tray, drizzle over some olive oil, and roast for 35–40 minutes, or until golden and tender. Meanwhile, bring a large saucepan of salted water to a boil. Add the parsnip and cauliflower and cook for 15–20 minutes until tender. Drain

½ head of cauliflower (about 1½ pounds / 680 g), florets cut into 2-inch (5-cm) pieces
1 teaspoon lemon juice
½ teaspoon ground turmeric
1 tablespoon coconut cream

and shake off any excess water. Place the cooked parsnip and cauliflower in a food processor. Cut the roasted garlic in half horizontally and squeeze in the soft garlic flesh. Add the oil, lemon juice, turmeric, and coconut cream and process until smooth. Season with salt and pepper to taste.

7. To assemble the pies, fill six 13½ fluid ounce (400 ml) capacity ovenproof dishes with the curried meat mixture, leaving ¾ inch (2 cm) space at the top. Top with the mash and spread out evenly. Place the dishes on a baking tray and bake for 15–20 minutes, or until the pies are heated through.

8. Spoon the mustard seed oil over the top and finish with the Crispy Curry Leaves.

MY MEATLOAF

SERVES: 6–8

Prep Time: 20 minutes **Cook Time:** 50 minutes (plus 10 minutes resting time)

8 slices free-range bacon, rind removed
1 large yellow onion, diced
1 small carrot, finely diced
2 celery stalks, finely chopped
2 cloves garlic, crushed
½ zucchini, finely diced
1¾ pounds (800 g) grass-fed ground beef
4 tablespoons almond meal
4 tablespoons chopped flat-leaf parsley leaves
2 organic, free-range eggs, lightly whisked
1 tablespoon sea salt
½ tablespoon freshly cracked black pepper
2 tablespoons coconut oil or other good-quality fat
4 tablespoons tomato ketchup (sugar-free and gluten-free)
1 tablespoon honey, *optional*
1 tablespoon apple cider vinegar

1. Preheat the oven to 350°F (180°C).
2. Line the base and sides of a loaf tin with a piece of parchment paper, cutting into the corners to fit and allowing the paper to extend 2 inches (5 cm) above the sides. Line the base and sides of the prepared tin with five slices of bacon, reserving the remaining rashers for the top.
3. Heat a skillet over medium heat with 2 tablespoons of coconut oil. Add the onion, carrot, and celery and cook for 5 minutes until softened, then add the garlic and zucchini and cook for a further 3 minutes. Drain out any excess liquid and allow the vegetables to cool completely in a colander.
4. Place the ground beef, almond meal, parsley, cooked vegetables, eggs, salt, and pepper in a bowl and mix until well combined.
5. Pack the meat mixture firmly into the lined loaf tin, and lay the remaining bacon slices over the top, tucking them in so they don't overhang from the sides.
6. Bake in the oven for 25 minutes.
7. Meanwhile to make the glaze, mix the tomato ketchup, honey (if using), and vinegar in a small bowl. Remove the meatloaf from the oven and baste the top of the meatloaf with the glaze. Return to the oven and continue cooking for a further 25 minutes, or until cooked through. To test if the meatloaf is cooked, insert a thermometer into the center of the meatloaf—it should reach at least 160°F (70°C).
8. Allow the meatloaf to rest in a warm place for 10 minutes before turning out of the tin—this will also allow the meat to reabsorb any cooking liquids. Slice and serve with your favorite salad or roasted vegetables.

ITALIAN SAUSAGE WITH SAUTÉED GREENS

SERVES: 6

Prep Time: 12–15 minutes **Cook Time:** 20 minutes

ALMOND DRESSING

⅓ cup (80 ml) extra-virgin olive oil

⅓ cup (60 g) almonds (activated if possible), toasted and chopped

2 tablespoons apple cider vinegar or lemon juice

1 teaspoon Dijon mustard

2 tablespoons salted baby capers, rinsed well and patted dry

2¼ pounds (1 kg) Italian sausage, not linked if possible (ask your butcher)

3 tablespoons melted coconut oil or good-quality animal fat, *divided*

1½ bunches of broccolini (about 9 ounces / 250 g)

1 bunch of lacinato kale (also known as cavolo nero, about 10.5 ounces / 300 g), stems discarded and leaves torn into large pieces

Sea salt and freshly ground black pepper

1. Preheat the outdoor grill to medium–hot or large skillet over medium heat.
2. Combine all the dressing ingredients in a bowl with some salt and pepper and mix well. Set aside until needed.
3. Roll the sausage into a tight round, then insert a metal skewer through the sausage from one side to the other. Turn the sausage and insert another skewer to form a cross. This secures the sausage and makes it easy to turn when cooking. Brush both sides of the sausage with 1 tablespoon of the coconut oil or fat.
4. Grill the sausage, turning over every 2–3 minutes, for 10–12 minutes until golden brown and cooked through. Transfer to a board or platter.
5. Meanwhile, combine the broccolini and cavolo nero in a bowl, add the remaining coconut oil or fat, and toss until well coated.
6. Heat a large skillet over medium heat or the barbecue hotplate to medium. Add the broccolini and kale and sauté for 2 minutes. Pour 3 tablespoons of water over the greens, toss, and cook for a further 2–3 minutes until wilted and cooked through. Season with salt and pepper.
7. Transfer the sautéed greens to a serving dish, spoon over the dressing, and serve with the sausage.

BRAISED LAMB SHOULDER WITH MASH

SERVES: 6

Prep Time: 15 minutes **Cook Time:** about 6–6½ hours

- **3⅓ pounds (1.5 kg) lamb shoulder, bone in, scored with a sharp knife**
- **2 tablespoons coconut oil or good-quality animal fat, *divided***
- **Sea salt and freshly ground black pepper**
- **2 yellow onions, finely chopped**
- **4 cloves garlic, finely chopped**
- **2 carrots, diced**
- **2 teaspoons finely chopped rosemary leaves**
- **1 tablespoon ground cumin**
- **2 cups (480 ml) Beef Bone Broth (page 238) or water, plus more if needed**
- **14 ounces (400 g) whole peeled tomatoes (see Note)**

TO SERVE

- **Parsnip Mash (page 98)**
- **Chopped flat-leaf parsley leaves**

1. Preheat the oven to 285°F (140°C) or 250°F (120°C convection/fan-forced).
2. Coat the lamb with 1 tablespoon of the coconut oil or fat, then rub evenly with salt and pepper.
3. Heat ½ tablespoon of the coconut oil or fat in a large flameproof casserole dish over medium–high heat. Sear the lamb for 2 minutes each side, or until well browned. Remove the lamb from the dish and set aside until needed.
4. Reduce the heat to medium, add the remaining coconut oil or fat to the dish, then add the onions and cook, stirring occasionally, for 5–8 minutes until softened. Add the garlic, carrots, and rosemary and cook for 5 minutes, or until slightly softened. Stir in the cumin and cook for 1 minute, or until fragrant. Pour in the broth and tomatoes and bring to a boil, then remove from the heat and season with salt and pepper.
5. Return the lamb shoulder to the dish and press down to submerge in the liquid, adding more broth or water if needed. Cover the dish with a tight-fitting lid, or tightly seal with at least two layers of foil so no steam can escape. Transfer to the oven to braise for 5½–6 hours until the meat pulls away easily from the bone. If there is any resistance, the lamb needs to be cooked for a little longer.
6. Carefully remove the lamb from the dish, cover with foil, and set aside to rest. Place the dish over medium heat, bring the juices to a simmer, and reduce for 12–15 minutes, or until it reaches a sauce consistency. Return the lamb to the dish

Note:

I prefer to buy diced and whole peeled tomatoes in jars rather than cans, due to the presence of bisphenol A (BPA) in some cans. BPA is a toxic chemical that can interfere with our hormonal system.

and simmer for a further 5 minutes, or until it is heated through. Season to taste with salt and pepper.

7. Divide the lamb among serving plates, add a couple of big spoonfuls of mash, then ladle over the sauce and sprinkle on the parsley.

MEXICAN BEEF AND VEGETABLE SOUP

SERVES: 6

Prep Time: 15–20 minutes **Cook Time:** 2½ hours

- **2 tablespoons coconut oil or good-quality animal fat, *divided***
- **1½ pounds (700 g) grass-fed blade steak (or another cut of beef that is good for stewing), cut into 1-inch (2.5-cm) cubes**
- **2 yellow onions, chopped**
- **4 cloves garlic, finely chopped**
- **1 red chili pepper, such as Fresno or red jalapeño, deseeded and chopped, *optional***
- **2 carrots, cut into ¾-inch (2-cm) cubes**
- **2 teaspoons Mexican spice blend**
- **1 teaspoon ground cumin**
- **1 can (14 ounces / 400 g) whole peeled tomatoes, crushed**
- **5 cups (1.25 liters) Beef or Chicken Bone Broth (page 238 or 239)**
- **2 zucchini (about 250 g), halved lengthwise and sliced**
- **2 yellow squash, chopped**
- **9 ounces (250 g) broccoli, broken into small florets**
- **Sea salt and freshly ground black pepper**
- **Cilantro leaves, to serve**

1. Heat 1 tablespoon of the coconut oil or fat in a large, heavy-based saucepan over medium–high heat. Add the beef in batches and cook for 3 minutes on all sides until browned. Transfer to a plate and set aside.
2. Reduce the heat to medium, add the remaining oil or fat and the onions to the pan and sauté for 5 minutes, or until softened. Stir in the garlic and chili (if using) and sauté for 30 seconds, or until fragrant. Add the carrots, spice blend, cumin, tomatoes, and broth, then return the beef to the pan and stir. Bring to a boil, then reduce the heat to low, cover with a lid, and simmer for 1½ hours.
3. Add the zucchini, squash, and broccoli to the soup and simmer, uncovered, for a further 30 minutes, or until the beef is very tender. Season with salt and pepper.
4. Ladle the soup into warm bowls, top generously with cilantro leaves, and serve.

SPICY PORK LARB

SERVES: 4

Prep Time: 15 minutes **Cook Time:** 8 minutes

- **2 tablespoons coconut oil or good-quality animal fat**
- **2 cloves garlic, finely chopped**
- **1 lemongrass stem, pale part only, finely chopped**
- **1⅓ pounds (600 g) ground pork**
- **⅓ cup (80 ml) lime juice**
- **2 tablespoons fish sauce, plus extra if needed**
- **1–2 red Thai chilies, deseeded and finely chopped**
- **2 kaffir lime leaves, finely chopped**
- **1 scallion, finely sliced**
- **1 handful mint leaves**
- **1 handful cilantro leaves**
- **1 small handful Thai basil leaves**
- **2 red Asian shallots, finely sliced**
- **8 savoy cabbage leaves, trimmed into cups**
- **1 Persian cucumber, sliced**
- **1 cup (100 g) Crispy Pork Crackling (page 68), chopped**
- **Lime wedges, to serve**

1. Heat the coconut oil or fat in a large, heavy-based skillet over medium–high heat. Add the garlic and lemongrass and stir-fry for 30 seconds, or until fragrant. Add the ground pork and cook, stirring with a wooden spoon to break up the lumps, for 6 minutes, or until browned and crumbly. Stir in the lime juice, fish sauce, chili, lime leaves, and scallions. Remove from the heat and leave to cool for 1 minute.
2. Toss half the mint, cilantro, Thai basil, and shallot through the ground pork. Taste and add a little more fish sauce if needed.
3. Spoon into the cabbage cups and add the cucumber, then scatter over the pork crackling, the remaining herbs, and shallot.
4. Serve with lime wedges on the side.

CARNE ASADA WITH FLATBREADS

SERVES: 4

Prep Time: 30 minutes (plus 2 hours or overnight marinating time)
Cook Time: 15 minutes (plus 5 minutes resting time)

MARINADE

⅓ cup (80 ml) olive oil
3 tablespoons tamari or coconut aminos
1 teaspoon ground cumin
4 cloves garlic, finely grated
3 tablespoons lime juice
2 tablespoons apple cider vinegar
1 tablespoon honey, *optional*
1 teaspoon freshly ground black pepper
2 jalapeño peppers, deseeded and finely chopped (leave the seeds in if you like it hot)
3 tablespoons finely chopped cilantro leaves

2¼ pounds (1 kg) grass-fed flank steak or sirloin steak
2 tablespoons coconut oil or good-quality animal fat
Sea salt and freshly ground black pepper
8 Flatbreads (page 282)
1 cup (¼ head) shredded iceberg lettuce
¾ cup (200 g) Cashew Sour Cream (page 258)
1 handful cilantro sprigs
Lime halves, to serve

1. Combine all the marinade ingredients in a large, shallow bowl. Add the steak to the marinade and turn to coat. Cover and refrigerate for at least 2 hours or, for best results, overnight. Flip the steak over halfway to evenly marinate.
2. When ready to cook, heat an outdoor flat-top grill to medium–hot or place a large, heavy-based skillet over medium–high heat and brush with the coconut oil or fat.
3. Season the steak with salt and pepper. Cook the steak on one side, basting with the marinade from time to time, for 6 minutes until charred, then flip and cook for a further 5–6 minutes for medium–rare, or cook to your liking. Place the steak on a plate and rest for 5 minutes, keeping warm.
4. Place the remaining marinade in a saucepan over medium–low heat. Cook, stirring occasionally, for 3 minutes until heated through.
5. Place all the guacamole ingredients in a bowl and mix gently. Season with salt and pepper and set aside.
6. Mix the tomato salsa ingredients in a bowl and season with salt and pepper.
7. Thickly slice the steak, arrange on a platter, and pour over the warm marinade. Serve with the flatbreads, guacamole, tomato salsa, iceberg lettuce, keto sour cream, cilantro sprigs, and lime halves, and let everyone help themselves.

GUACAMOLE

2 avocados, diced
1 tablespoon finely chopped cilantro leaves
2 tablespoons lime juice, or to taste
3 tablespoons olive oil

TOMATO SALSA

2 tomatoes, deseeded and cut into ½-inch (1-cm) cubes
¼ red onion, finely chopped
1 tablespoon finely snipped chives
1 tablespoon lime juice
2 tablespoons extra-virgin olive oil

CABBAGE AND BACON SOUP

SERVES: 4

Prep Time: 15 minutes **Cook Time:** 50 minutes

- **2½ tablespoons coconut oil or good-quality animal fat, *divided***
- **1 yellow onion, chopped**
- **2 cloves garlic, chopped**
- **10½ ounces (300 g) Swiss chard, leafy green part and stems separated, all trimmed and chopped**
- **10½ ounces (300 g) green cabbage, shredded**
- **7 ounces (200 g) rindless bacon**
- **½ teaspoon ground turmeric**
- **6½ cups (1.5 liter) Chicken Bone Broth (page 239)**
- **Sea salt and freshly ground black pepper**
- **1 large handful flat-leaf parsley leaves**

1. Melt 2 tablespoons of oil or fat in a large saucepan over medium heat. Add the onion and cook for 5 minutes, or until softened. Stir in the garlic, Swiss chard stems, and cabbage and cook for 5 minutes, or until softened.
2. Meanwhile, melt the remaining ½ tablespoon of oil or fat in a skillet over medium–high heat. Add the bacon and cook until lightly golden, about 2 minutes per side. Remove from the pan, reserving any fat in the pan.
3. Chop the bacon into ¾-inch (2-cm) pieces and stir into the cooked cabbage mixture, then add the turmeric, broth, and any bacon fat from the pan. Bring to a boil, reduce the heat to low, and gently simmer, stirring occasionally, for 30 minutes.
4. Stir in the chopped Swiss chard leaves and cook for a further 5 minutes until wilted. Season with salt and pepper. To finish, stir in the parsley leaves and serve.

HOMEMADE BACON

MAKES: 2.2 POUNDS (1 KG)

Prep Time: 15 minutes (plus 1 week to marinate) **Cook Time:** 2½ hours

2.2 pounds (1 kg) free-range pork belly
3 tablespoons sea salt
2 tablespoons liquid smoke, *optional*
1 tablespoon freshly ground black pepper
2 teaspoons finely chopped rosemary leaves
1 teaspoon finely chopped thyme leaves
1 teaspoon fennel seeds
2 cloves garlic, chopped
2 tablespoons honey, *optional*

1. Rinse the pork belly in cold water and pat dry with paper towel.
2. Place the pork in a large dish and set aside. To make the marinade, place the salt, liquid smoke (if using), pepper, rosemary, thyme, fennel seeds, and garlic in a mortar and pound with a pestle to finely crush. Stir through the honey (if using) to combine.
3. Rub the marinade over the pork belly until completely coated. Cover and refrigerate for 1 week, flipping the pork every day.
4. Remove the pork from the dish, scrape off the marinade, and rinse thoroughly in cold water.
5. Pat the pork dry with a clean cloth.
6. Preheat the oven to 195°F (90°C). Place a lightly greased wire rack on a baking sheet. Place the cured pork belly, skin-side down, on the wire rack and roast for 2–2½ hours, or until the internal temperature of the pork reaches 149°F (65°C). Remove from the oven and cool slightly.
7. When cool enough to handle, transfer the pork to a cutting board and slice off the skin. Place the skin in an airtight container in the refrigerator and reserve for making crackling. Set the bacon aside at room temperature and allow to cool completely, then place in a container, cover, and refrigerate for a few hours. Slice to your preferred thickness.
8. Place the bacon slices in a skillet over medium heat and cook for a few minutes on each side until golden brown and crispy. Enjoy with eggs and your favorite sides, or add to any dishes you like. Store the remaining bacon in an airtight container in the fridge for up to 2 weeks or freeze for up to 3 months.

BRAISED SHORT RIBS AND PICKLES

SERVES: 4–6

Prep Time: 10 minutes **Cook Time:** 8 hours

- **4½ pounds (2 kg) grass-feed beef short ribs, at room temperature**
- **2 cups (480 ml) Beef Bone Broth (page 238)**
- **3 tablespoons coconut oil or good-quality animal fat**
- **Sea salt and freshly ground black pepper**
- **3 tablespoons Barbecue Spice Blend (page 262), plus ½ teaspoon extra for the mayonnaise**
- **1 cup (200 g) finely sliced dill pickles**
- **¾ cup (200 g) Mayonnaise (page 244)**

1. Preheat the oven to 250°F (120°C) or 210°F (100°C convection/fan-forced).
2. Rub the coconut oil or fat into the short ribs and season with salt and pepper.
3. Heat a large flameproof casserole dish over medium–high heat. Add the beef and cook for 5 minutes on each side to brown. Set aside to cool a little.
4. When the beef is cool enough to handle, rub all over with the barbecue spice blend. Return to the dish, pour in the broth and cover with the lid. Transfer to the oven to braise for 8 hours, or until the beef is meltingly tender and falling off the bone.
5. Mix the extra ½ teaspoon of barbecue spice blend into the mayonnaise.
6. Gently place the ribs on a platter, ladle over some broth, and serve with the pickles and spicy mayonnaise on the side.

SIRLOIN STEAK WITH CARAMELIZED ONION AND ARUGULA SALAD

SERVES: 4

Prep Time: 8 minutes **Cook Time:** 15 minutes (plus 5 minutes resting time)

- **4 (5½-ounce) (150 g) sirloin steaks, at room temperature**
- **2 yellow onions, sliced**
- **2 large handfuls baby arugula leaves**
- **1 handful basil leaves (or micro basil)**
- **3 tablespoons, melted coconut oil or good-quality animal fat**
- **2 teaspoons Steak Seasoning (page 264)**
- **Sea salt and freshly ground black pepper**
- **3 tablespoons Italian Dressing (page 252)**

1. Heat an outdoor grill plate to hot or a large grill pan over high heat.
2. Brush the steaks with 1 tablespoon of the coconut oil or fat and season with a good pinch of steak seasoning. Cook the steaks on one side for 4 minutes, or until golden brown, then flip and cook for a further 3 minutes for medium–rare (or cook to your liking). Transfer to a plate and rest for 4–5 minutes, keeping warm.
3. Reduce the heat to medium–high and add the remaining coconut oil or fat to the grill or pan. Add the onion and sauté for 7–8 minutes until softened and starting to caramelize. Season with salt and pepper.
4. Place the arugula and basil in a bowl, add the dressing and toss to lightly coat the leaves. Season the salad with a little salt and pepper to taste.
5. Place the steaks on serving plates, sprinkle over a little more steak seasoning, then serve with the caramelized onion and arugula salad.

SHEPHERD'S PIE

SERVES: 6

Prep Time: 25 minutes (plus 1 hour soaking time if using lambs' brains)
Cook Time: 40 minutes

- **1 large head of cauliflower (about 3 pounds / 1.36 kg), chopped into florets**
- **4 tablespoons coconut oil or other good-quality fat, *divided***
- **1 teaspoon ground cumin**
- **1 yellow onion, diced**
- **4 cloves garlic, crushed**
- **2 celery stalks, diced**
- **2 carrots, diced**
- **1⅓ pounds (600 g) grass-fed ground beef**
- **2 lambs' brains, soaked in cold water with 1 teaspoon salt added for 1 hour, rinsed well and finely chopped, *optional***
- **2½ tablespoons tomato paste**
- **1 teaspoon thyme leaves, chopped**
- **4 tablespoons red wine (such as Shiraz), *optional***
- **1½ cups (375 ml) Beef Bone Broth (page 238)**
- **Sea salt and freshly ground black pepper**
- **3 tablespoons roughly chopped flat-leaf parsley leaves**
- **Seasonal salad, to serve**

1. Preheat the oven to 350°F (180°C).
2. Fill a large saucepan with water and bring to a boil, then add the cauliflower and cook until the cauliflower is tender, about 10 minutes. Drain the cooked cauliflower in a colander and set aside.
3. Heat 2 tablespoons of oil or fat in a large, deep skillet over medium–high heat. Add the cumin, onion, garlic, celery, and carrots and cook for 5 minutes, or until the vegetables are softened and beginning to brown. Add the ground beef and brains (if using) and cook, stirring to break up any lumps, until browned. Add the tomato paste and thyme and cook for 1 minute, then pour in the wine and bone broth and simmer for 10 minutes, stirring occasionally. Season with salt and pepper.
4. Meanwhile, place the cooked cauliflower in the bowl of a food processor and process until smooth. Add the remaining oil or fat and puree, then season with salt and pepper.
5. To assemble, spread the meat mixture into the base of an ovenproof dish and level with a spoon. Cover with the cauliflower puree and smooth the top out evenly. Bake for 30 minutes, or until the top is lightly golden. Sprinkle with the parsley and serve with a fresh salad of your choice.

LAMB BURGERS WITH CHERMOULA

SERVES: 4

Prep Time: 25 minutes **Cook Time:** 20 minutes

CHERMOULA

3 tablespoons roughly chopped mint leaves

3 tablespoons roughly chopped flat-leaf parsley leaves

1 tablespoon finely grated lemon zest

2 cloves garlic, roughly chopped

½ teaspoon smoked paprika

½ teaspoon red pepper flakes

3 tablespoons extra-virgin olive oil

2 tablespoons lemon juice

Sea salt and freshly ground black pepper

2 tablespoons coconut oil or good-quality animal fat, *divided*

½ yellow onion, finely chopped

2 cloves garlic, finely chopped

1¼ pounds (560 g) grass-fed ground lamb

3½ ounces (100 g) minced lamb, pork, or beef fat (ask your butcher), *divided*

3½ ounces (100 g) free-range chicken livers or lamb liver, finely chopped

1 tablespoon ras el hanout spice blend

Sea salt and freshly ground black pepper

1. Combine all the chermoula ingredients in a mortar and pound to a paste with a pestle.
2. Heat 1 tablespoon of the coconut oil or fat in a skillet over medium heat. Add the onion and sauté for 5 minutes, or until softened. Stir in the garlic and cook for 1 minute, or until fragrant. Transfer to a bowl and allow to cool completely.
3. Add the ground lamb, fat of choice, liver, ras el hanout, 1 teaspoon of salt, and ½ teaspoon of pepper to the cooled onion mixture, then mix well. Shape the mixture into eight patties.
4. Heat a large, heavy-based skillet over medium–high heat. Add the remaining oil or fat and cook the patties in batches for 3 minutes on each side until cooked through. Transfer to a plate and rest for 2 minutes, keeping warm.
5. Arrange the patties on a platter, drizzle over the chermoula, and serve.

MAHA POULTRY: VERSATILITY ON A PLATE

Gather 'round for chicken done MAHA style, where every bite feels like a warm embrace. This chapter's bursting with dishes that make your taste buds dance—think crispy roast chicken, zesty grilled wings, or a comforting pot of my mum Joy's chicken and vegetable soup. Here, we don't care about the clock. That spicy drumstick you love at lunch? It's just as perfect for breakfast. Dreaming of a chicken salad at dawn? Make it happen. Using affordable cuts and simple ingredients, these recipes turn humble chicken and poultry into something extraordinary, celebrating quality and flavor without breaking the bank. Whether you're tossing wings on the grill or slow-cooking a cozy meal, this is about creating moments that linger. So, set the table, light some candles, and let's cook chicken that's as flexible and joyful as your day demands.

CHINESE LEMON ROAST CHICKEN DRUMSTICKS

SERVES: 4

Prep Time: 10 minutes (plus marinating time) **Cook Time:** 45 minutes

2½ pounds (1.13 kg) chicken drumsticks, skin on
4 scallions, julienned, white and green parts separated
½ lemon, cut into wedges
2 heads garlic, halved
Fresh cilantro leaves, for serving
1 tablespoon toasted sesame seeds, for serving
3 tablespoons tamari sauce
1 tablespoon Shaoxing wine
3 tablespoons honey
1 tablespoon coconut oil, melted

LEMON SAUCE

2 cloves garlic, minced
½ tablespoon finely grated fresh ginger
½ cup (120 ml) chicken broth
2 tablespoon lemon juice
1 teaspoon finely grated lemon zest
3 tablespoons tamari sauce
3 tablespoons honey
2 teaspoon tapioca flour, mixed with 1 tablespoon cold water
2½ teaspoon sesame oil
1 tablespoon finely chopped cilantro
Sea salt and cracked pepper

1. In a large bowl, combine the chicken drumsticks with tamari, Shaoxing wine, honey, and melted coconut oil. Toss well to coat evenly. Cover and marinate in the refrigerator for at least 2 hours or overnight.
2. Preheat the oven to 400°F (200°C).
3. When the chicken is marinated, scatter the white parts of the scallions in a roasting pan. Arrange the marinated drumsticks on top, pour over the remaining marinade from the bowl, then add the halved garlic heads and lemon wedges around the chicken.
4. Place in the oven and roast for 30 minutes. Flip the drumsticks over, then continue roasting for another 15 minutes, or until the chicken is cooked through and dark golden brown.
5. While the chicken is roasting, combine all the sauce ingredients in a small saucepan and stir to combine. Bring to a gentle simmer over medium-low heat and cook 5 minutes. Season with sea salt and freshly cracked pepper.
6. **To serve:** Remove the chicken from the oven. Sprinkle with the green parts of the scallions, fresh cilantro leaves, and toasted sesame seeds. Serve with the lemon sauce and cauliflower rice.

CHICKEN LIVER PARFAIT

SERVES: 6–8

Prep Time: 20 minutes **Cook Time:** 45 minutes (plus chilling time)

- 1 pound (450 g) organic, free-range chicken livers, cleaned and trimmed
- 2 shallots, finely chopped
- 2 cloves garlic, finely chopped
- 1½ teaspoons fresh thyme leaves
- 1 cup (240 ml) duck fat or ghee, softened (plus extra melted for sealing)
- ⅓ cup (80 ml) Chicken Bone Broth (page 239)
- 3 tablespoons coconut cream
- Sea salt and freshly ground black pepper
- Melted duck fat or ghee, for sealing

TO SERVE

- Toasted paleo bread (page 281)
- Cornichons or dill pickles
- Sauerkraut (page 268)

1. Rinse the chicken livers under cold water, trim off any sinew, and pat them dry thoroughly with paper towels.
2. In a skillet over medium heat, melt 1 tablespoon of duck fat or ghee. Add the shallots, garlic, and thyme, and cook for 3–4 minutes, until softened and fragrant but not browned. Remove from the pan and set aside.
3. Return the pan to medium-high heat. Add 1 tablespoon of duck fat or ghee, then add the chicken livers and cook for 4–5 minutes, until browned on the outside but still pink and tender in the center.
4. Pour in the chicken bone broth to deglaze the pan, stirring to loosen any browned bits. Remove from the heat and let cool for 5 minutes.
5. Transfer the chicken livers and any pan juices to a food processor. Add the reserved shallot mixture and the remaining duck fat or ghee, and blend until completely smooth.
6. Add the coconut cream, season generously with sea salt and black pepper, and blend again until silky and light.
7. For an ultra-smooth texture, pass the mixture through a fine mesh sieve into a bowl or jug.
8. Divide the parfait among ramekins or jars, smoothing the tops with a spatula.
9. Pour a thin layer of melted duck fat or ghee over the surface to seal.
10. Chill for at least 4 hours, preferably overnight, until fully set.
11. Serve cold with toasted paleo bread, cornichons or dill pickles, and sauerkraut.

GREEN CHICKEN CURRY WITH BROCCOLI AND CAULIFLOWER RICE

SERVES: 4

Prep Time: 25 minutes **Cook Time:** 25 minutes

2 tablespoons coconut oil or good-quality animal fat
1.3 pounds (600 g) boneless, free-range skinless chicken thighs, cut into ¾-inch (2-cm) cubes
1 yellow onion, finely chopped
2 cloves garlic, crushed or minced
4 tablespoons green curry paste
1⅔ cups (400 ml) coconut cream
¾ cup (180 ml) chicken broth
1 tablespoon green peppercorns (in brine, drained)
2 kaffir lime leaves, torn
Fish sauce, to taste
1 large handful green beans, trimmed
1 head broccoli, cut into florets
Cauliflower Rice, to serve (page 286)
Fresh cilantro sprigs, for garnish
Lime wedges, for serving

1. In a large wok or deep skillet, heat the coconut oil over high heat. Working in batches, add the chicken and stir-fry for about 5 minutes until golden all over. Transfer the cooked chicken to a bowl and set aside, reserving the oil in the pan.
2. Return the wok or skillet to medium-high heat with the reserved oil. Add the onion and garlic, and stir-fry for 1 minute until fragrant and slightly softened.
3. Stir in the green curry paste and cook for another minute, stirring constantly, until fragrant.
4. Return the chicken and any juices to the pan. Pour in the coconut cream and chicken broth, then add the green peppercorns and kaffir lime leaves. Bring to a boil, then reduce heat to medium-low and simmer uncovered for 10 minutes, allowing the flavors to develop and the sauce to slightly thicken.
5. Taste and season with fish sauce as desired.
6. Meanwhile, steam the green beans in a steamer basket for about 2 minutes, or until tender-crisp. Add the steamed beans to the curry and stir to combine.
7. Steam the broccoli florets for about 5 minutes, or until tender-crisp.
8. Prepare the cauliflower rice according to recipe (page 286).
9. Divide the cauliflower rice among serving bowls. Ladle over the green chicken curry with green beans and top with steamed broccoli. Garnish with fresh cilantro sprigs and serve with lime wedges on the side.

CHICKEN AND CUCUMBER WELLNESS BOWL

SERVES: 4

Prep Time: 10–15 minutes **Cook Time:** n/a

2 Persian cucumbers

DRESSING

1 tablespoon toasted sesame oil
3 tablespoons extra-virgin olive oil
3 tablespoons lime juice
2 teaspoons tamari
1 teaspoon Dijon mustard
Sea salt and freshly ground black pepper

1 baby romaine lettuce, trimmed and leaves torn
2 baby bok choy, trimmed and shredded
1 celery stalk, finely sliced
7 ounces (200 g) Chinese or Napa cabbage, shredded
2 scallions, finely sliced
⅔ cup (100 g) sauerkraut
1 pound (450 g) leftover roast chicken, shredded
2 tablespoons sesame seeds, toasted
1 handful cilantro leaves
1 long red chili, finely chopped, *optional*

1. Use a vegetable peeler or mandoline to slice the cucumbers into ribbons; discard the seedy core.
2. Combine all the dressing ingredients in a bowl and mix well. Taste and add more salt and pepper if needed.
3. Arrange the cucumber ribbons, romaine lettuce leaves, bok choy, celery, cabbage, scallions, and sauerkraut in serving bowls. Top with the chicken, pour the dressing over the top, then scatter on the sesame seeds and cilantro leaves, and sprinkle on the chili (if using).

CHINESE EGG DROP SOUP

SERVES: 4

Prep Time: 10 minutes **Cook Time:** 20 minutes

- **1 quart (1 liter) Chicken Bone Broth (page 239)**
- **2 free-range chicken thighs**
- **1½-inch (4-cm) piece of ginger, finely julienned**
- **2 scallions, sliced, white and green parts separated**
- **2 teaspoons tamari or coconut aminos, or to taste**
- **2 organic, free-range eggs, lightly beaten**
- **Sea salt and freshly ground black pepper**
- **1 teaspoon toasted sesame seeds, to serve**
- **Sesame oil, to serve**

1. Bring the chicken broth to a simmer in a saucepan over medium heat. Add the chicken, ginger, scallion whites, and tamari or coconut aminos and cook for 15 minutes, or until the chicken is cooked through. Remove the chicken thighs from the broth and, when cool enough to handle, shred into pieces.
2. Return the chicken to the broth, bring to a simmer, and then slowly pour in the beaten eggs while stirring in one direction. Simmer for a further 30 seconds. Season with salt and pepper, if needed.
3. To serve, ladle the soup into bowls, sprinkle with the scallion greens and toasted sesame seeds, and drizzle over a little sesame oil.

BUFFALO WINGS

SERVES: 4

Prep Time: 15–20 minutes (plus, 2 hours or overnight to marinate) **Cook Time:** 15 minutes

MARINADE

1/3 cup (80 ml) melted lard, tallow, or duck fat (page 277)
1 teaspoon ground cumin
1 teaspoon garlic powder
1 teaspoon onion powder
2 teaspoons finely grated ginger
1 tablespoon smoked paprika
1 tablespoon honey
1½ tablespoons apple cider vinegar
½ teaspoon fine sea salt
Pinch freshly ground black pepper

2½ pounds (1.1 kg) chicken wings
Coconut oil, for deep-frying
1 cup (120 g) tapioca flour
Sea salt and freshly ground black pepper
2/3 cup (150 ml) Hot Sauce (page 247)

1. Combine the marinade ingredients in a large bowl and whisk together well.
2. Toss the wings in the marinade and turn to coat well. Cover and marinate in the fridge for 2 hours or, for best results, overnight.
3. Heat the coconut oil in a wok or large saucepan to 320°F (160°C). (To test, drop a small piece of chicken into the oil—if it starts to bubble around the chicken immediately, the oil is ready.)
4. Place the tapioca flour in a shallow bowl and season with salt and pepper. One at a time, add the chicken wings, turn to coat, and shake well to dust off any excess flour.
5. Carefully add the wings in batches to the hot oil and deep-fry for 6 to 6½ minutes until cooked through and golden. Remove with a slotted spoon and place on paper towel to drain. Season with salt and pepper.
6. Transfer the wings to a bowl, pour over the hot sauce and toss the chicken to evenly coat.
7. Arrange the buffalo wings on a platter and serve.

CHICKEN AND ASPARAGUS STIR-FRY

SERVES: 4–6

Prep Time: 25 minutes **Cook Time:** 20 minutes

- **3 tablespoons coconut oil or other good-quality fat, *divided***
- **1¾ pound (800 g) free-range chicken thigh fillets, skin on if possible, cut into ⅓-inch (1-cm) slices**
- **6 cloves garlic, finely chopped**
- **2-inch (5-cm) piece ginger, finely julienned**
- **1 long red chili, deseeded and finely sliced, *optional* (for less heat)**
- **2 bunches asparagus (about 12 spears), trimmed, cut lengthways, then cut diagonally into 2-inch (5-cm) lengths**
- **3 scallions, white parts cut lengthways, then cut into 2-inch (5-cm) pieces, green parts thinly sliced**
- **⅓ cup (80 ml) Shaoxing wine or dry white wine**
- **½ cup (120 ml) chicken broth**
- **2 tablespoons tamari sauce**
- **1 teaspoon sesame oil**
- **2 teaspoons sesame seeds**
- **2 teaspoons honey or coconut sugar**
- **1 tablespoon tapioca flour, mixed with 2 tablespoons water**
- **2 bunches Chinese broccoli (about 10 ounces / 280 g), trimmed and roughly chopped**
- **Sea salt and freshly ground black pepper, to season**

TO SERVE

Cauliflower Rice (page 286)

1. Heat 1 tablespoon of coconut oil in a wok or large heavy-based skillet over high heat. Working in batches, sauté the chicken slices for 5–6 minutes, or until just browned and cooked through. Transfer to a plate and set aside.
2. Add another 1 tablespoon coconut oil to the wok. Add the garlic, ginger, and chili. Stir-fry for 1½ minutes until fragrant.
3. Add the asparagus and the white parts of the green onions. Stir-fry for 1½ minutes, or until just starting to brown.
4. Add the Chinese broccoli and continue to stir-fry for 2 minutes, or until they reach your preferred level of tenderness.
5. Return the cooked chicken to the pan. Pour in the Shaoxing wine (or white wine), chicken broth, and tamari sauce. Add the honey or coconut sugar, sesame oil, sesame seeds, and season with freshly ground black pepper. Bring to a simmer.
6. Stir in the tapioca flour slurry and bring to a boil. Simmer for 2 minutes, or until the sauce has thickened slightly. Taste and season with salt and pepper as needed.
7. Divide the cauliflower rice among four serving bowls. Spoon the stir-fry over the rice, and sprinkle with the thinly sliced green onion tops to serve.

JAMAICAN JERK CHICKEN

SERVES: 4

Prep Time: 25 minutes (overnight to marinate) **Cook Time:** 30 minutes

2¼ pounds (1 kg) free-range chicken drumsticks
2 bay leaves
2 tablespoons coconut oil lime wedges, to serve
1 handful cilantro leaves, to serve
Roasted Vegetables, to serve (page 191)

JERK MARINADE

1 red onion, chopped
3 scallions, chopped
6 large cloves garlic, crushed
4 scotch bonnets or habanero chilies, deseeded and chopped
3 tablespoons lime juice
3 tablespoons tamari or coconut aminos
3 tablespoons coconut oil, melted
1 tablespoon white wine vinegar
1 tablespoon honey, *optional*
1 tablespoon thyme leaves
1 tablespoon paprika
2 teaspoons ground allspice
2 teaspoons freshly ground black pepper
1½ teaspoons sea salt
½ teaspoon ground cinnamon
¼ teaspoon freshly grated nutmeg

1. To make the jerk marinade, combine all the ingredients in a food processor and process to a smooth paste.
2. Transfer the marinade to a large shallow bowl, add the chicken and bay leaves, and turn the chicken to coat. Cover and refrigerate overnight for best results.
3. Preheat the oven to 400°F (200°C).
4. Bring the chicken to room temperature 20 minutes before cooking.
5. Heat the oil in a large skillet over medium–high heat. Add the chicken drumsticks, in batches, and sear, basting occasionally with the marinade, for 5 minutes, or until browned on all sides. Place the chicken in a roasting tin and roast in the oven for 20–25 minutes, or until the chicken is cooked all the way through. Cover with foil and allow to rest for 5 minutes before serving. Remove bay leaves.
6. Arrange the chicken and lime wedges on a platter and sprinkle over the cilantro leaves. Serve with roasted vegetables.

J

BRAISED GINGER CHICKEN

SERVES: 4–6

Prep Time: 20 minutes **Cook Time:** 65 minutes

- 1 whole chicken (about 4 pounds /1.8 kg), cut into 8 pieces
- 1 tablespoon tapioca flour, *optional*
- 3 tablespoons coconut oil or good-quality animal fat, melted
- 1 yellow onion, chopped
- 4 cloves garlic, finely sliced
- 2-inch (5-cm) piece of ginger, cut into thin strips
- Sea salt and freshly ground black pepper
- ½ cup (120 ml) dry white wine
- 1 cup (240 ml) Chicken Bone Broth (page 239)
- 1 tablespoon fish sauce
- 1 tablespoon tamari or coconut aminos
- 3 long red chilis, deseeded and finely sliced (leave some seeds in if you like it spicy)
- 4 scallions, cut into thin strips
- 1 bunch bok choy (about 10½ ounces / 300 g), trimmed
- Lightly toasted sesame seeds, to serve

1. Preheat the oven to 320°F (160°C).
2. Place the chicken pieces in a large bowl, add the tapioca flour (if using), and toss to coat.
3. Melt the oil or fat in a large roasting pan or an oven-safe skillet over medium–high heat. Add the onion and cook, stirring occasionally, for 5 minutes until translucent. Stir in the garlic and ginger and cook for 1 minute until fragrant. Add the chicken pieces, skin-side down, season with salt and pepper, and cook for 3 minutes until lightly golden.
4. Pour in the wine, broth, fish sauce, and tamari or coconut aminos and scatter on the chili and scallions.
5. Cover tightly with a double layer of foil and braise in the oven for 45 minutes.
6. Remove the chicken from the oven and mix in the bok choy. Cover and return to the oven for 15 minutes until the chicken is cooked through.
7. Season the sauce if needed. Sprinkle the sesame seeds over the braised chicken and serve with a side of Asian greens.

MEXICAN CHICKEN WITH ROASTED PUMPKIN AND AVOCADO AND TOMATO SALSA

SERVES: 4

Prep Time: 35–45 minutes **Cook Time:** 1¼–1½ hours

1 butternut squash (about 4–4½ pounds / 1.8–2 kg), halved lengthwise, deseeded
2 tablespoons coconut oil or good-quality animal fat, melted
Sea salt and freshly ground black pepper
1 scallion, finely sliced
1 handful cilantro leaves
3 tablespoons sliced pickled jalapeño chili
Lime wedges, to serve

MEXICAN CHICKEN

2 tablespoons coconut oil or good-quality animal fat
2 yellow onions, finely chopped
2 cloves garlic, finely chopped
1 tablespoon chipotle chilies in adobo sauce, chopped, plus extra if desired
1½ pounds (700 g) free-range boneless chicken thighs, skin off, cut into ½-inch (1-cm) thick strips
1 teaspoon smoked paprika, plus extra to serve
1 teaspoon ground cumin
½ teaspoon ground coriander
1½ tablespoons tomato paste

1. Preheat the oven to 350°F (180°C) or 320°F (160°C fan-forced/convection).
2. Brush the butternut squash with the coconut oil or animal fat. Place, cut-side up, in a roasting pan and sprinkle with salt and pepper. Roast for 1¼–1½ hours until tender.
3. Meanwhile, to make the Mexican chicken, heat the coconut oil or animal fat in a large skillet over medium–high heat. Add the onion and cook for 5 minutes, or until softened. Stir in the garlic and chipotle chili and cook for 1 minute, or until fragrant. Add the chicken and sauté for 5 minutes, or until browned. Add the spices and tomato paste and cook for 1 minute, then mix in the tomatoes and broth. Reduce the heat to medium–low and simmer for 15 minutes, or until the chicken is cooked through and the sauce has thickened. Season with salt and pepper. If you like things a little spicier, add some extra chipotle chili.
4. Mix the avocado and tomato salsa ingredients in a bowl and season with salt and pepper.
5. Carefully transfer the roasted butternut squash to two serving plates. Spoon the Mexican chicken over the squash, then top with the avocado and tomato salsa. Finish with a sprinkle of scallions, cilantro, pickled jalapeño chili, and a pinch of smoked paprika, and serve with the lime wedges.

14 ounces (400 g) whole peeled tomatoes, crushed (see Note)
⅔ cup (150 ml) Chicken Bone Broth (page 239) or water

AVOCADO AND TOMATO SALSA

1 avocado, sliced
2 tomatoes, deseeded and cut into ½-inch (1-cm) dice
¼ red onion, finely chopped
1 long red chili, deseeded and finely chopped
2 tablespoons lime juice
2 tablespoons extra-virgin olive oil

Note:

I prefer to buy diced and whole peeled tomatoes in jars rather than cans, due to the presence of bisphenol A (BPA) in some cans. BPA is a toxic chemical that can interfere with our hormonal system.

SOUTHERN FRIED CHICKEN

SERVES: 4

Prep Time: 30 minutes **Cook Time:** 30 minutes

SPICE MIX

3 tablespoons psyllium husks
¼ cup (30 g) tapioca flour
2 cups (200 g) almond meal
2 teaspoons dried oregano
2 teaspoons dried basil
½ teaspoon chili powder
2 teaspoons freshly ground black pepper
2 teaspoons sea salt
1 teaspoon sweet paprika
2 teaspoons ground cumin
2 teaspoons garlic powder
2 teaspoons onion powder

4 organic, free-range eggs
2 tablespoons almond milk
1⅓ cup (150 g) hemp or tapioca flour, for coating
4-pound (1.8 kg) chicken, cut into 10 pieces
Coconut oil or good-quality animal fat, for deep-frying
¾ cup (200 g) Aioli (page 245)
⅓ cup (80 ml) Hot Sauce (page 247)
Sea salt
Lemon wedges, to serve

1. Preheat the oven to 355°F (180°C) or 320°F (160°C convection/fan-forced).
2. Place all the spice mix ingredients in a shallow bowl and mix well.
3. Whisk the eggs and almond milk in another shallow bowl. Place the hemp or tapioca flour in a third bowl.
4. One at a time, toss the chicken pieces in the flour and dust off the excess. Then dip in the egg mixture, followed by the spice mixture, turning and pressing gently to coat thoroughly.
5. Add enough coconut oil or animal fat to fill a large saucepan by one-third and heat to 320°F (160°C) over medium–high heat. (To test, drop a small piece of chicken into the oil—it should bubble instantly around the edges.) Add the chicken in batches and fry for 3–4 minutes until golden. Remove with a slotted spoon and drain on paper towel. Transfer the chicken to a baking sheet and roast for 10–15 minutes until cooked through.
6. Spoon the aioli into a small serving bowl, then swirl through the hot sauce.
7. Season the chicken with salt and serve with the aioli dipping sauce and the lemon wedges on the side.

CRISPY CHICKEN SALAD WITH TOASTED WALNUTS

SERVES: 4

Prep Time: 20 minutes **Cook Time:** 12 minutes (plus 5 minutes to rest)

4 free-range boneless chicken thighs, skin on
Sea salt and freshly ground black pepper
1 tablespoon coconut oil or good-quality animal fat
Extra-virgin olive oil, for drizzling

DRESSING

⅓ cup plus 1 tablespoon (90 g) Mayonnaise (page 244)
1½ tablespoons lemon juice
¼ teaspoon grated garlic

SALAD

4½ cups (400 g) shredded savoy cabbage
2 large handfuls of baby spinach leaves
½ red onion, finely chopped
1 pink lady apple, cored and cut into matchsticks
1 handful mint leaves, torn
1 handful flat-leaf parsley leaves
1 handful chervil leaves
1 handful tarragon leaves
1 cup (100 g) toasted walnuts

1. To make the crispy chicken, pat the chicken thighs dry with paper towel, then place between two sheets of parchment paper and flatten with a meat mallet. Season the skin with 2 teaspoons of salt.
2. Heat the coconut oil or fat in a large heavy-based skillet over medium–high heat. Add the chicken thighs, skin-side down, and season the exposed flesh with a little salt. Fry, undisturbed, for 6–8 minutes until the skin is crispy and golden brown. Turn and cook for 3–4 minutes until cooked through. Transfer the chicken, skin-side up, to a wire rack and leave to rest for 5 minutes. Chop into bite-sized pieces.
3. To make the dressing, place the mayonnaise, lemon juice, garlic, and 2 teaspoons of water in a small bowl and mix to combine. Season with salt and pepper.
4. Arrange all the salad ingredients in a large bowl, top with the chicken, then pour over the dressing. Drizzle over some olive oil and season with salt and pepper. Give the salad a good toss before eating.

CHICKEN LIVER CURRY

SERVES: 4

Prep Time: 15–20 minutes **Cook Time:** 30 minutes

PANCH PHORAN (INDIAN FIVE-SPICE BLEND)

- 1 tablespoon cumin seeds
- 1 tablespoon brown or yellow mustard seeds
- 1 tablespoon fennel seeds
- 1 tablespoon nigella seeds
- 1½ teaspoons fenugreek seeds

- 1¾ pounds (800 g) free-range chicken livers
- 3 tablespoons coconut oil or good-quality animal fat, *divided*
- 1½ yellow onions, finely chopped
- 30 fresh curry leaves
- 2 teaspoons finely grated ginger
- 2 cloves garlic, finely chopped
- 3 tablespoons curry powder
- 1½ tomatoes, chopped
- 1 green chili pepper (such as serrano or jalapeño), deseeded and finely chopped (keep the seeds in if you like it spicy)
- 2 cups (480 ml) Chicken Bone Broth (page 239) or water
- Sea salt and freshly ground black pepper
- Handful cilantro leaves

1. Combine the panch phoran ingredients in a bowl. Set aside until ready to use.
2. Rinse the chicken livers under cold water, pat dry with paper towels, and trim off any fat, sinew, and veins. Set aside.
3. Heat 2 tablespoons of the coconut oil or fat in a large, deep skillet over medium–high heat. Add the chicken livers in batches and seal for 30 seconds on each side. Remove from the pan and set aside.
4. Add the remaining oil or fat to the pan and place over medium heat. Add the onions and sauté for 8 minutes, or until softened and starting to color. Immediately add 1½ teaspoons of panch phoran and the curry leaves and cook, stirring frequently, for 20 seconds, or until fragrant.
5. Reduce the heat to medium–low, add the ginger and garlic, and cook for 1 minute, then add the curry powder, tomatoes, and chili and cook, stirring occasionally, for 6 minutes, or until the tomato has broken down. Stir in the broth, bring to a simmer for 8 minutes, then add the chicken livers. Reduce the heat to low and simmer for a further 4–6 minutes until the chicken livers are just cooked through and the sauce is thick and fragrant.
6. Season with salt and pepper, sprinkle the cilantro, and serve.

Tip:

Store the leftover panch phoran in an airtight container in the pantry for up to 3 months.

KOREAN CHICKEN MEATLOAF WITH KIMCHI AND SSAMJANG GLAZE

SERVES: 6

Prep Time: 25 minutes **Cook Time:** 45 minutes (plus 10 minutes resting time)

MEATLOAF

- 1⅓ pounds (600 g) free-range ground chicken
- 1 pound (450 g) free-range ground pork
- ¾ cup (160 g) kimchi (for a recipe, see page 266), plus extra to serve
- 2 tablespoons coconut oil
- 1 red onion, finely chopped
- 1 tablespoon finely grated ginger
- 3 cloves garlic, finely chopped
- ½ cup (50 g) almond meal
- 2 tablespoons finely chopped cilantro leaves
- 1 organic, free-range egg
- 1 tablespoon tamari or coconut aminos
- 2 teaspoons sesame oil
- 1 teaspoon sea salt
- ¼ teaspoon freshly ground black pepper

SSAMJANG GLAZE

- 1 tablespoon sriracha
- 1 tablespoon apple cider vinegar
- 2 tablespoons honey
- 1½ teaspoons finely grated ginger
- 1 tablespoon tomato paste

GARNISH

- 2 scallions, finely sliced
- 1 tablespoon sesame seeds, toasted

1. Preheat the oven to 350°F (180°C). Line the base and sides of a 5 × 8-inch (12 cm × 20-cm) loaf pan with a piece of parchment, cutting into the corners to fit and allowing the paper to extend 2 inches (5 cm) above the sides.
2. Place all the meatloaf ingredients in a bowl and mix until well combined. Firmly pack the meat mixture into the prepared pan, then bake in the oven for 25 minutes.
3. Meanwhile, to make the ssamjang glaze, combine all the ingredients in a bowl and mix well.
4. Remove the meatloaf from the oven and baste the top with half the glaze. Return to the oven and bake for 20 minutes until cooked through. To test if the meatloaf is cooked, insert a thermometer into the center; if it reaches at least 160°F (70°C), it's ready.
5. Allow the meatloaf to rest in a warm place for 10 minutes before turning out of the pan. Spoon over the remaining glaze, then sprinkle on some kimchi, scallions, and sesame seeds. Slice and serve with your favorite salad or roasted vegetables.

ROGAN JOSH CHICKEN

SERVES: 4–6

Prep Time: 20 minutes **Cook Time:** 35 minutes

4 tablespoons coconut oil
1 yellow onion, chopped
5 cloves garlic, chopped
1½ tablespoons finely grated ginger
½ teaspoon ground cloves
1½ teaspoons ground turmeric
1 teaspoon ground cardamom
1 teaspoon fennel seeds
2 teaspoons ground coriander
2 teaspoons ground cumin
2 teaspoons paprika
½ teaspoon chili powder
2 cinnamon sticks
2 bay leaves
14½-ounce (400-g) can or jar whole peeled tomatoes, crushed (or 14½ ounces/400 g fresh tomatoes, diced)
3 tablespoons Chicken Bone Broth (page 239)
Sea salt and freshly ground black pepper
2 pounds (900 g) free-range chicken thigh fillets, cut into ¾ -inch (2-cm) pieces
Juice of ½ lemon

TO SERVE

Cilantro leaves
Cauliflower Rice (page 286)
Raita (page 252)
1 long green chili, finely sliced

1. Heat the coconut oil in a large saucepan over medium heat. Add the onion and sauté for 5 minutes until translucent. Reduce the heat to low and stir in the garlic, ginger, spices, and bay leaves and cook, stirring frequently, for 3 minutes. Add the tomatoes and cook for 1 minute, then pour in the broth and mix well. Season with salt and pepper.
2. Increase the heat to medium and bring the sauce to a simmer. Add the chicken and stir until well coated with the sauce.
3. Cover the pan with a lid, reduce the heat to low and cook, stirring occasionally, for 20–25 minutes until the chicken is cooked through and the sauce has thickened. Remove bay leaves.
4. Stir the lemon juice into the curry, scatter on the cilantro leaves and serve with the cauliflower rice, raita, and chili.

PAD SEE EW

SERVES: 4

Prep Time: 15 -20 minutes **Cook Time:** 12 minutes

5 carrots (about 1 pound / 480 g)
2 tablespoons coconut oil
6 cloves garlic, finely chopped
$1\frac{1}{3}$ pounds (600 g) free-range chicken breast or thigh fillets, thinly sliced on the diagonal
1 pound (450 g) broccolini, chopped into 2-inch (5-cm) lengths
4 tablespoons tamari or coconut aminos
2 organic, free-range eggs

TO SERVE

Thai basil leaves
Sliced scallions
Black and white sesame seeds
Lime wedges

1. To make the carrot noodles, use the wide ribbon blade on a vegetable spiralizer. Alternatively, place the carrots on a chopping board and, using a vegetable peeler, peel into thin, wide ribbons. (Save the leftover trimmings for broths or soups.)
2. Melt the oil in a wok or deep skillet over medium heat. Add the garlic and chicken and stir-fry for 2 minutes until the chicken changes color.
3. Add the broccolini and tamari or coconut aminos to the pan and cook for 5 minutes until the broccolini is softened. Add the carrot noodles and stir-fry for another 3 minutes.
4. Push the stir-fry aside in the pan. Crack in the eggs, stir vigorously to scramble them and cook for 2 minutes until set. Mix everything together and serve immediately with the basil leaves, scallions, sesame seeds scattered over the top, and the lime wedges on the side.

ROASTED TURKEY WITH HERB MARINADE

SERVES: 8

Prep Time: 30–40 minutes—plus 24 hours to marinate **Cook Time:** 3¼ hours

MARINADE

2 large handfuls of mint leaves
2 large handfuls of curly parsley leaves
2 large handfuls of cilantro leaves
4 cloves garlic, peeled
1 cup (240 ml) lemon juice
1 cup (240 ml) white wine
1 cup (240 g) good-quality fat, melted
2 teaspoons ground cumin
Salt and freshly ground black pepper

8-pound (3.6-kg) whole turkey
Good-quality fat, melted
2 carrots, sliced lengthways
1 yellow onion, sliced
4 cloves garlic, peeled
5 fresh bay leaves
1⅓ quarts (1.25 liters) chicken bone broth (to make your own, see page 239)
2 tablespoons tapioca flour, mixed with 3 tablespoons water

STUFFING

2 tablespoons good-quality fat, melted
1 yellow onion, finely chopped
4 garlic confit cloves (to make your own, see page 278)
3 slices of bacon, diced
4 tablespoons chopped curly parsley
3 tablespoons dukkah
1 pound (450 g) free-range ground pork
1 teaspoon finely grated lemon zest

1. To make the marinade, combine all the ingredients in a food processor and blend until smooth. Put the turkey in a large shallow dish, pat dry with paper towels, and pour the marinade over. Massage the marinade all over the turkey and inside the cavity, cover with plastic wrap, and place in the fridge for 24 hours. Every few hours massage the marinade onto the bird.

2. The next day, remove the turkey from the fridge and allow to come to room temperature (this will take about 1 hour). Preheat the oven to 465°F (240°C).

3. To make the stuffing, heat the fat in a saucepan over medium heat. Add the onion and cook until soft, about 5 minutes. Crush the garlic confit and add to the pan, along with the bacon. Cook until just starting to color, about 3–5 minutes. Remove from the heat and set aside to cool. Add the remaining ingredients and mix until combined.

4. Fill the turkey cavity with the stuffing, then cross the legs over and tie with kitchen string. Place in a large roasting pan and pour in the marinade. Rub with some melted fat and season with salt and pepper. Add the carrots, onion, garlic, and bay leaves, cover with foil, and place in the oven. Reduce the temperature to 350°F (180°C) and roast, pouring the pan juices over the turkey a few times, for about 2 hours. To brown the skin, remove the foil in the final 40 minutes. The turkey is cooked once the juices run clear when the inside of the thigh is pierced with a skewer. Cooking time may vary—it should take about 15 minutes

per pound (40 minutes per kilogram). Transfer the turkey to a large serving platter, cover with foil and rest for 20 minutes.

5. To make the gravy, place the chicken stock in a saucepan over medium heat and simmer until reduced by half, about 20 minutes. Skim the fat from the surface of the juices in the roasting pan with the vegetables and discard. Pour the tapioca mixture and stock into the roasting pan and mix well. Bring to a boil over medium heat, stirring occasionally. Reduce the heat to low and simmer until the sauce thickens. Strain into a gravy boat or bowl. Carve the turkey and serve with the gravy. For a whole Thanksgiving feast, serve with Roasted Veg (page 191), Whole Roasted Cauliflower (page 196), or Spiced Butternut Squash Soup (page 199).

MAHA SEAFOOD: A SPLASH OF COASTAL JOY

Dive into the vibrant world of MAHA's fish and seafood, where every dish feels like a seaside escape. Picture a nourishing bowl of wild salmon curry, succulent shrimp tossed in a ginger stir fry, or a colorful seafood chowder brimming with tantalizing flavors. This chapter celebrates the ocean's bounty, turning sustainable catches into unforgettable meals. From crispy pan-fried fillets to delicate oysters kissed with a Spanish dressing, these recipes are crafted to spark delight and bring people together. Whether you're grilling wild fish fillets for a crowd or whipping up a quick fish salad for a quiet dinner, it's about savoring the moment. So, dust off your favorite skillet, let the kitchen hum with creativity, and dive into dishes that transform simple ingredients into coastal magic. Let's make waves at the table with every bite.

STEAMED WILD SALMON WITH SCALLIONS AND GINGER

SERVES: 4

Prep Time: 10 minutes **Cook Time:** 10 minutes

4 (5½-ounce/160 g) wild salmon fillets, skin on, pin-boned
Sea salt and freshly ground black pepper
3 cups (700 ml) Chinese broth (page 241)
8 scallions, white and green parts cut into 3-inch (8-cm) lengths
2-inch (5-cm) piece ginger, cut into matchsticks, plus extra to serve
Micro cilantro leaves, to serve, *optional*

1. Season the salmon with salt and pepper.
2. Line a steamer basket with a sheet of parchment paper. Fill a saucepan with water, bring to a boil, then reduce the heat to low. Place the salmon in the steamer, cover, and steam for 3–4 minutes until the fish is still a slightly deeper pink in the center and almost cooked through. Transfer to a plate and allow to rest for 2 minutes, keeping warm.
3. Meanwhile, combine the broth, scallions, and ginger in a saucepan and place over medium–low heat. Bring to a gentle simmer and cook for 5 minutes, or until the scallions are tender. If needed, season with a little salt.
4. To serve, ladle the broth, scallions, and ginger into warm serving bowls. Add the steamed salmon fillets, then finish with the extra ginger and micro cilantro (if using).

PALEO FISH PIE WITH SWEET POTATO MASH & PINE NUT HERB CRUMB

SERVES: 4

Prep Time: 30 minutes **Cook Time:** 35 minutes

SWEET POTATO MASH

- **1½ pounds (700 g) sweet potatoes, peeled and chopped**
- **2 tablespoon melted ghee or extra-virgin olive oil**
- **Pinch sea salt**
- **Freshly ground black pepper, to taste**
- **2 tablespoons arrowroot or tapioca flour, mixed with 3 tablespoons cold water to make a slurry**

SEAFOOD FILLING

- **1½ tablespoons coconut oil or good-quality fat (such as ghee, lard, or tallow)**
- **1 yellow onion, finely chopped**
- **3 cloves garlic, finely chopped**
- **1 leek, chopped**
- **½ cup (125 ml) Chicken Bone Broth or Fish Bone Broth (pages 239 and 241)**
- **1 cup (240 ml) coconut cream**
- **2 teaspoons baby capers**
- **1 tablespoon seeded mustard or Dijon mustard**
- **1 pound (450 g) white fish, skin removed (e.g. Alaskan cod, bream, bass, or snapper), cut into 1-inch (2½-cm) pieces**
- **5⅓ ounces (150 g) raw shrimp, peeled and deveined, halved**

1. Make the sweet potato mash: Place the sweet potatoes in a saucepan and cover with water. Bring to a boil and cook for about 20 minutes, or until soft. Drain well, then mash with ghee or olive oil. Season with salt and pepper. Set aside.
2. Prepare the seafood filling: Heat coconut oil in a large skillet over medium heat. Add the onion, garlic, and leek, and cook for 4–5 minutes until soft and fragrant. Stir in the broth, followed by the coconut cream. Add the capers and mustard, and simmer for 3–4 minutes, until slightly thickened. Gently fold in the fish, shrimp, and scallops. Cook for 3–4 minutes, or until just opaque. Stir in the parsley, lemon juice, salt, and pepper. Finally, add the arrowroot slurry and stir until thickened. Remove from heat.
3. Assemble the pie: Preheat the oven to 375°F (190°C). Spoon the seafood filling into a baking dish or individual ramekins. Top with the sweet potato mash, spreading evenly.
4. Bake for 20–25 minutes, or until golden and bubbling.
5. Meanwhile to make the pine nut crumb: Heat the ghee in a small skillet over medium heat. Add the pine nuts and toast, stirring often, for 1 minute until lightly golden. Add the garlic and lemon zest and cook for 30 seconds. Stir in the parsley, season lightly with salt, and remove from heat.

6 scallops, chopped
1 tablespoon flat-leaf parsley, chopped
1½ tablespoons lemon juice
Sea salt and freshly ground black pepper, to taste

PINE NUT & HERB CRUMB

1 tablespoon ghee
½ cup (70 g) pine nuts
2 tablespoons flat-leaf parsley, finely chopped
1 clove garlic, finely chopped
1 teaspoon lemon zest

6. Allow to cool, then place the nut mixture in a food processor and pulse a few times to finely chop or chop finely with a knife.
7. To serve: Sprinkle the pies with the pine nut and herb crumb and serve with green salad on the side.

FISH AND CHIPS WITH SWEET POTATO FRIES

SERVES: 4

Prep Time: 20 minutes **Cook Time:** 30 minutes

SWEET POTATO FRIES

2 large sweet potatoes (about 1.75 pounds/ 800 g), peeled and cut into fries
Coconut oil or fat, for deep-frying
Sea salt, to season

4 (6.3–7-ounce/180–200-g) firm white fish fillets (such as snapper, bass, whiting, sole, John Dory), skin on or off
Tapioca flour, for coating
Sea salt and freshly ground black pepper
4 tablespoons ghee or high-quality animal fat, for pan-frying

TO SERVE

Mixed salad leaves (mesclun)
Lemon wedges
Aioli or mayonnaise

1. **To prepare the sweet potato fries:** Peel the sweet potatoes and cut into thin batons or fries. Rinse under cold water, then pat thoroughly dry with a clean towel. Heat coconut oil or fat in a deep fryer or heavy saucepan to 350°F (180°C). Fry the sweet potato in batches for 3–5 minutes, or until golden and crisp. Remove with a slotted spoon and drain on paper towels.
2. Meanwhile, lightly coat the fish fillets in tapioca flour, shaking off the excess. Season both sides with salt and pepper.
3. Heat the ghee or animal fat in a large skillet over medium-high heat. Add the fish fillets, skin-side down (if using) and cook for 3 minutes on the first side, or until golden and crispy. Flip and cook for another 2–3 minutes, or until the fish is just cooked through and flakes easily.
4. Arrange the fish and fries in serving baskets or plates. Add a handful of mesclun salad, a lemon wedge, and a dollop of aioli or mayonnaise on the side. Serve immediately.

ASIAN MUSHROOMS WITH FISH

SERVES: 4

Prep Time: 10–15 minutes **Cook Time:** 8 minutes

- **2 tablespoons coconut oil or good-quality animal fat**
- **2 cloves garlic, finely chopped**
- **1 tablespoon finely grated ginger**
- **2 scallions, finely chopped**
- **7 ounces (200 g) shiitake mushrooms, finely sliced**
- **1 tablespoon apple cider vinegar**
- **1 tablespoon tamari or coconut aminos**
- **1 teaspoon fish sauce, plus extra if needed**
- **2 cups (500 ml) Fish or Chicken Bone Broth (pages 241 and 239)**
- **4 (6-ounce/160-g) fish of your choice (such as snapper fillets, or bream, sea bass, Spanish mackerel), skin on, each fillet halved**
- **Sea salt**
- **1½ teaspoons sesame seeds, toasted**
- **1 handful cilantro leaves**
- **Olive oil, to serve**

1. Heat the coconut oil or animal fat in a large skillet over medium–high heat. Add the garlic, ginger, and scallions and sauté for 10 seconds. Stir in the shiitake mushrooms and continue to sauté for 2 minutes, or until softened.
2. Pour the vinegar, tamari or coconut aminos, and fish sauce into the pan and cook for 30 seconds, then pour in the broth. Bring to a boil, then reduce the heat to low, add the fish pieces, cover with the lid, and simmer for 2½–3 minutes until the fish is cooked through. If needed, add a splash more fish sauce or a little salt for seasoning.
3. Sprinkle the sesame seeds and cilantro over the fish, drizzle with olive oil, and serve.

GINGER SHRIMP

SERVES: 2- 4

Prep Time: 15 minutes **Cook Time:** 10 minutes

- 3 tablespoons coconut oil or good-quality animal fat, *divided*
- 1⅓ pounds (600 g) raw shrimp, shelled and deveined, tails left intact
- 2-inch (5-cm) piece of ginger, cut into fine matchsticks
- 4 scallions, white parts chopped, green parts finely shredded
- 4 cloves garlic, finely chopped
- 2 red long chili, finely sliced
- ⅓ cup (80 g) gluten-free oyster sauce
- 1 tablespoon fish sauce
- 2 teaspoons coconut sugar
- 1 cup (250 ml) Chicken Bone Broth (page 239)
- Sea salt and freshly ground black pepper
- 1 handful Thai basil leaves

1. Heat 1 tablespoon of the coconut oil or animal fat in a wok or skillet over medium–high heat. Add the shrimp in batches and cook for 15 seconds on each side. Remove from the pan and set aside.
2. Wipe the pan clean, add the remaining oil or fat, and place over medium–high heat. Add the ginger, scallion whites, garlic, and chili and stir-fry for 2 minutes, or until fragrant and starting to color slightly.
3. Combine the oyster sauce, fish sauce, coconut sugar, and broth in a bowl, then pour into the pan and stir. Simmer for 1–2 minutes, or until the sauce thickens.
4. Return the shrimp to the pan, add the scallion greens, and toss for about 30 seconds until the shrimp are just cooked. Remove from the heat, season with salt and pepper, toss through the Thai basil leaves, and serve.

WILD SALMON WITH MINTED PEA PUREE AND LEMON BROTH

SERVES: 4

Prep Time: 10–15 minutes **Cook Time:** 30 minutes

LEMON BROTH

- 1 tablespoon coconut oil or good-quality animal fat
- 3½ ounces (100 g) speck, finely chopped
- 2 shallots, chopped
- 2 cups (480 ml) Chicken Bone Broth (page 239)
- 1 teaspoon finely grated lemon zest
- 3 teaspoons lemon juice
- Sea salt and freshly ground black pepper

MINTED PEA PUREE

- 2⅓ cup (350 g) frozen peas, thawed
- 1 large handful mint leaves
- 3 roasted garlic cloves
- 3 tablespoons olive oil

- 4 (5½-ounce/160-g) wild salmon fillets, skin on, pin-boned
- 2 tablespoons coconut oil or good-quality animal fat
- 1 tablespoon chopped mint leaves, plus extra leaves to serve

1. Preheat the oven to 400°F (200°C) or 355°F (180°C fan-forced/convection).
2. To make the lemon broth, heat the coconut oil or animal fat in a saucepan over medium heat. Add the speck and shallots and cook for 5 minutes, or until lightly golden and softened. Pour in the broth, then stir though the lemon zest. Bring to a boil, reduce the heat to low, and gently simmer for 10 minutes to allow the flavors to infuse. Stir in the lemon juice and season with salt and pepper.
3. Meanwhile, to make the minted pea puree, bring a saucepan of salted water to a boil. Add the peas and cook for 3 minutes, or until tender. Drain, reserving 2½ tablespoons of cooking water. Combine the peas, mint, garlic, and reserved cooking water in a food processor and process to a puree. With the motor running, pour in the olive oil in a slow, steady stream and process until combined. Season with salt and pepper. Set aside, keeping warm.
4. Heat a large ovenproof skillet over high heat until very hot. Brush the salmon fillets with the coconut oil or animal fat, season with salt and pepper and cook, skin-side down, for 30–60 seconds until crispy. Transfer the pan to the oven and cook the salmon, still skin-side down, for 3½–4 minutes until the skin is golden and crisp (or cook to your liking). Flip the fillets, skin-side up, onto a plate and allow to rest for 2–3 minutes, keeping warm. At this point the salmon will be perfectly cooked; slightly pink and moist in the middle.
5. To serve, stir the mint into the lemon broth, then ladle the hot broth into shallow serving bowls. Spoon in a good dollop of pea puree, then top with the salmon.

OYSTERS WITH JAMON VINAIGRETTE

SERVES: 4

Prep Time: 10 minutes **Cook Time:** n/a

JAMON VINAIGRETTE

1 French shallot, finely chopped
2¾ ounces (80 g) serrano jamon (or prosciutto), finely diced
⅓ cup (80 ml) red wine vinegar
⅓ cup (80 ml) extra-virgin olive oil
1 teaspoon finely snipped chives
Sea salt and freshly ground black pepper

24 oysters, freshly shucked

1. To make the vinaigrette, place the shallot, jamon, vinegar, olive oil, and chives in a bowl and mix to combine. Season with salt and pepper.
2. Arrange the oysters on a platter of ice and top each one with a spoonful of vinaigrette.

WILD SALMON POKE BOWL

SERVES: 4

Prep Time: 20–25 minutes **Cook Time:** n/a

DRESSING

3 tablespoons tamari
1 garlic clove, finely grated
1 teaspoon finely grated ginger
2 teaspoons yuzu juice or lemon juice
1½ teaspoons Sriracha Chili Sauce (page 250)
2 teaspoons toasted sesame oil
3 tablespoons olive oil or avocado oil

7 ounces (200 g) daikon (white radish), cut into matchsticks
6½ ounces (180 g) red cabbage, finely shredded
6½ ounces (180 g) savoy cabbage, finely shredded
1 avocado, sliced
1 Persian cucumber, thinly sliced
1 pound (450 g) sashimi-grade salmon, cut into ½-inch (1-cm) cubes
1 teaspoon shichimi togarashi, or to taste, *optional*
1 tablespoon Furikake Seasoning (page 262)
2 tablespoons salmon roe
⅓ cup (80 g) Mayonnaise (page 244)
1 handful cilantro leaves
Baby shiso leaves or micro herbs of your choice, *optional*

1. Place all the dressing ingredients in a bowl and whisk to combine.
2. Divide the daikon and cabbage among four serving bowls, then top with the avocado, cucumber, and salmon. Sprinkle over the shichimi togarashi (if using) and furikake, add the salmon roe, and finish with the mayonnaise, cilantro, and micro herbs. Pour over the dressing and eat immediately.

PAN-FRIED SNAPPER WITH BROCCOMOLE

SERVES: 4

Prep Time: 15–20 minutes **Cook Time:** 12–15 minutes

4 snapper fillets (about 5½ ounces / 160 g each), skin on or off, pin-boned
Sea salt and freshly ground black pepper
1 teaspoon lemon thyme leaves, chopped
2 tablespoons coconut oil
1 cup (150 g) sauerkraut
1 large handful watercress sprigs
4 lemon wedges, to serve

BROCCOMOLE

3½ ounces (100 g) broccoli, broken into florets
1 avocado, diced or mashed
⅛ red onion, finely chopped
1 clove garlic, finely chopped
1 tablespoon lime juice
½ teaspoon crushed red pepper flakes, *optional*
1 tablespoon extra-virgin olive oil, plus extra for drizzling
1 tablespoon chopped cilantro leaves

1. Season the snapper fillets with salt and pepper and sprinkle over the thyme.
2. Heat the coconut oil in a large heavy-based skillet over high heat. Fry the fish, skin-side down and in batches if necessary, for 2½–3 minutes, or until crispy. Flip over and cook for 2 minutes, or until the fish is just cooked through. Rest for 2 minutes.
3. To make the broccomole, bring a saucepan of salted water to a boil. Add the broccoli and cook for 3 minutes, or until just tender. Drain, then plunge the broccoli into ice-cold water to stop the cooking process. When the broccoli is completely cold, drain again, shake off any excess water, and chop into small pieces.
4. Place the avocado, onion, garlic, lime juice, crushed red pepper flakes (if using), olive oil, cilantro, and broccoli in a serving bowl and mix well. Season with salt and pepper.
5. To serve, divide the fish among four plates. Add the broccomole, sauerkraut, and watercress, and drizzle with a little extra olive oil. Serve with the lemon wedges.

SEAFOOD CHOWDER

SERVES: 4

Prep Time: 20 minutes **Cook Time:** 50 minutes

1½ tablespoons coconut oil or good-quality animal fat, *divided*
7 ounces (200 g) rindless bacon, diced
2 carrots, diced
2 celery stalks, diced
1 yellow onion, chopped
3 cloves garlic, finely chopped
1 turnip, diced
1 small sweet potato, diced
1 quart (1 liter) Fish or Chicken Bone Broth (pages 239 and 241)
1 cup (240 ml) coconut cream
1 bay leaf and 4 thyme sprigs, tied into a bundle
1¼ pounds (550 g) mussels, scrubbed and debearded
10½ ounces (300 g) white fish fillets (such as snapper), chopped into bite-sized pieces
5⅓ ounces (150 g) scallop meat, roughly chopped
5½ ounces (200 g) roughly chopped, peeled and deveined raw shrimp
Sea salt and freshly ground black pepper
1 tablespoon chopped flat-leaf parsley leaves
Lemon wedges, to serve

1. Heat 2 teaspoons of the coconut oil or fat in a large saucepan over medium heat. Add the bacon and cook for 6–8 minutes until golden and crisp. Remove the bacon from the pan, reserving the oil. Place the bacon on a plate and set aside until needed.
2. Return the pan to medium heat, add the remaining coconut oil or fat, the carrots, celery, and onion and cook for 10 minutes, or until the onion is softened. Add the garlic and cook for 30 seconds, or until fragrant. Add the turnip and sweet potato and cook, stirring occasionally, for 5 minutes. Pour in the broth and coconut cream, add the herb bundle, then reduce the heat to medium–low and simmer for 20 minutes, or until the veggies are tender. Add the mussels, cover with a lid, and cook for 4 minutes, or until all the mussels open. Using tongs, remove the mussels from the pan and set aside.
3. Carefully transfer half the stock and veggies to a blender. Blend until smooth, then return to the pan. Stir well, then add the fish and scallop meat, and stir again. Cook for a further 5 minutes.
4. Meanwhile, remove the mussels from their shells and roughly chop the meat. Add the mussel meat and shrimp to the chowder, stir well, and cook for a further minute until all the seafood is cooked through. Remove the herb bundle and season with salt and pepper.
5. Just before serving, stir in the bacon and parsley. Serve with lemon wedges for squeezing over.

NASI GORENG WITH SARDINES

SERVES: 2

Prep Time: 15–20 minutes **Cook Time:** 15 minutes

- **⅓ cup (80 g) duck fat or good-quality animal fat, *divided***
- **3 scallions, white and green parts separated, finely sliced**
- **1 carrot, finely chopped**
- **½ stalk celery, finely chopped**
- **4 cloves garlic, finely chopped**
- **2 teaspoons shrimp paste**
- **2 bird's eye chilies, deseeded and finely chopped (leave the seeds in if you like it hot), plus extra to serve if desired**
- **2 tablespoons chopped cilantro leaves, plus extra leaves to serve**
- **4 cups (720 g) uncooked Cauliflower Rice (page 286)**
- **1½ tablespoons tamari or coconut aminos**
- **2 teaspoons honey, *optional***
- **2 organic, free-range eggs**
- **Sea salt and freshly ground black pepper**
- **10 sardine fillets, skin on**
- **1 handful bean sprouts, rinsed and drained**
- **2 tablespoons Crispy Shallots (page 278), *optional***
- **Lime wedges, to serve**

1. Heat 2 tablespoons of the fat in a wok or large skillet over medium heat. Add the white part of the scallions, the carrot, and celery and stir-fry for 5 minutes, or until slightly softened. Stir in the garlic, shrimp paste, chili, and cilantro and fry for 1 minute, or until fragrant. Add the cauliflower rice, tamari or coconut aminos, and honey (if using) and continue to stir-fry for about 5 minutes, or until everything is combined and the cauliflower is cooked through.
2. Next, heat 1 tablespoon of fat in a nonstick skillet over medium heat. Crack in the eggs and cook for 2–2½ minutes until the egg whites have set, or cook to your liking. Season with some salt and pepper.
3. Meanwhile, heat the remaining fat in a large, heavy-based skillet over high heat. Season the sardine fillets with salt and pepper, then add them to the pan skin-side down and, in batches if necessary, and cook for 15 seconds. Flip and cook for a further 5 seconds, then remove from the pan.
4. Divide the fried cauliflower rice among serving bowls, top each with the sardines and an egg, then scatter over the green part of the scallions, the bean sprouts, cilantro leaves, and, if you like, some crispy shallots and extra chili. Serve with lime wedges on the side for squeezing over.

INDIAN FISH CURRY

SERVES: 4–6

Prep Time: 20 minutes, plus 10 minutes marinating time **Cook Time:** 25 minutes

2 teaspoons ground turmeric
2 teaspoons ground coriander
¼ teaspoon ground cardamom
1 teaspoon ground cumin
½ head cauliflower (about 14 ounces/ 400 g) broken into florets
1½ pounds (700 g) snapper, sea bass, bream fillets, or any white-fleshed fish of your choice, skin removed, cut into 1 ¼-inch (3-cm) pieces
¼ teaspoon sea salt
Juice of 1 lemon, *divided*
2 tablespoons coconut oil
1 yellow onion, chopped
1 tablespoon finely grated ginger
3 cloves garlic, finely chopped
1 cinnamon stick
½ teaspoon chili flakes
12 fresh curry leaves
Freshly ground black pepper
1 (13½-ounce/400-ml) can coconut cream
3 cups (750 ml) Fish Bone Broth (page 241)
1 long red chili, finely sliced, *optional*

1. Mix the ground turmeric, coriander, cardamom, and cumin in a small bowl and set aside.
2. Place the cauliflower in the bowl of a food processor and pulse into tiny, fine pieces that look like rice. Set aside.
3. Place the fish in a shallow bowl, season with salt, and pour on half the lemon juice. Cover with plastic wrap and place in the refrigerator to marinate for 10 minutes.
4. Meanwhile, melt the coconut oil in a large skillet over medium heat. Add the onion and sauté for 5 minutes, or until softened. Add the ginger and garlic and cook for 30 seconds, then stir in the spice mix, cinnamon, chili flakes, curry leaves, and a pinch of pepper and cook for 1 minute, or until fragrant. Pour the coconut cream and broth into the pan and bring to a simmer. Reduce the heat to low and cook for 10 minutes until the flavors infuse.
5. Stir in the cauliflower, add the fish, and simmer for 8–10 minutes until the fish is just cooked through.
6. To finish, season with salt, squeeze on the remaining lemon juice, and scatter on the chili (if using).

SARDINE AND COD LIVER PÂTÉ

SERVES: 4

Prep Time: 10 minutes (plus 2 hours to set) **Cook Time:** n/a

4¼ ounces (120 g) canned or jarred cod liver, drained
3¾ ounces (106 g) canned or jarred sardines in brine or olive oil, drained
⅓ cup (80 g) Mayonnaise (page 244)
1 teaspoon lemon juice
1 tablespoon olive oil
2 tablespoons coconut oil or good-quality animal fat
Sea salt and freshly ground black pepper
Crackers

1. Place the cod and sardines in the bowl of a food processor, then add the mayonnaise, lemon juice, olive oil, and coconut oil or fat and blend to a fine paste. Season with salt and pepper. Transfer to a serving bowl; cover and place in the fridge to set for 2 hours.
2. Sprinkle the pâté with a little freshly cracked pepper and serve with crackers of your choice.

GRILLED SARDINES WITH HERB & PRESERVED LEMON DRESSING

SERVES: 2–4

Prep Time: 25–30 minutes **Cook Time:** 2 minutes

HERB AND PRESERVED LEMON DRESSING

1/3 (80 ml) extra-virgin olive oil
1 tablespoon fresh oregano leaves, chopped
¼ teaspoon chili flakes
2 tablespoons finely chopped preserved lemon (rind only)
3 tablespoons flat-leaf parsley leaves, chopped
2 tablespoons lemon juice
1 clove garlic, finely chopped
Sea salt and freshly ground black pepper

10 whole sardines (about 1.1 pound / 500 g total), cleaned and rinsed (ask your fishmonger to do this)
1 tablespoon coconut oil or good-quality animal fat

SALAD

1 fennel bulb, shaved thinly
3 radishes, thinly sliced
1 avocado, diced
1 handful mint leaves
1 handful dill leaves
1 ruby red grapefruit, segmented
Juice of ½ lemon
2 tablespoons extra-virgin olive oil
Sea salt and freshly ground black pepper

1. To make the herb and preserved lemon dressing, combine the olive oil, chopped oregano, chili flakes, preserved lemon, parsley, lemon juice, garlic, and a generous pinch of salt and pepper in a small bowl. Stir well and set aside.
2. Brush the sardines with the coconut oil, then season with some salt and pepper.
3. Preheat an outdoor grill to high heat. Grill the sardines for 40–60 seconds on each side, or until just cooked through.
4. To prepare the salad, place the shaved fennel, sliced radishes, diced avocado, mint leaves, dill leaves, and grapefruit segments in a large bowl. Drizzle with the juice of ½ lemon and 2 tablespoons olive oil. Season with salt and pepper, then toss gently to combine.
5. Arrange the sardines on a serving platter and drizzle with the herb and preserved lemon dressing. Serve alongside the fennel, radish, and avocado salad.

MAHA VEGETABLES: NATURE'S VIBRANT PALETTE

Step into MAHA's vegetable haven, where fresh produce transforms into pure delight. Imagine roasted root veggies with a caramelized glow, crisp salads bursting with color, or a creamy spiced pumpkin soup that steals the show. This chapter celebrates the humble beauty of vegetables, turning farmers' market seasonal fresh finds into dishes that shine. From whole roasted cauliflower that looks like it belongs in a Michelin star restaurant to simply braised greens, every recipe invites creativity and connection at the table. Whether you're tossing a quick stir-fry or slow roasting a veggie-packed oven tray, these dishes make healthy eating a joy. Grab your favorite knife, let the kitchen buzz with energy, and let's craft vibrant, soulful meals that make vegetables the star.

ROAST VEG WITH NUTRITIONAL YEAST

SERVES: 4–6

Prep Time: 15 minutes **Cook Time:** 40 minutes

- 1 yellow onion, sliced
- 1 head of broccoli (about 10½ ounces / 300 g), stalk and florets thickly cut into 6–8 pieces
- 2 zucchini, thickly sliced diagonally
- 10½ ounces (300 g) savoy cabbage, cut into wedges
- 3 baby golden beets, halved lengthwise
- 1 garlic bulb, cloves separated
- 3 tablespoons coconut oil or good-quality animal fat
- Sea salt and freshly ground black pepper
- ½ cup (120 ml) Chicken Bone Broth (page 239)
- ½ bunch cavolo nero (about 5 ounces / 150 g), stems discarded and leaves torn (use the stems for broths or soups)
- 1 tablespoon chopped rosemary leaves
- 2 tablespoons nutritional yeast

1. Preheat the oven to 400°F (200°C) or 355°F (180°C fan-forced/convection). Line a large roasting pan with baking parchment paper.
2. Combine the onion, broccoli, zucchini, cabbage, beets, and garlic in the prepared pan; toss with the coconut oil or fat and season with salt and pepper.
3. Spread out the vegetables in a single layer, making sure they're not too bunched up. Pour in the broth and roast for 20 minutes. Add the cavolo nero and rosemary and roast for a further 20 minutes, or until the vegetables are tender and golden.
4. Arrange the roast vegetables on a platter, sprinkle over the nutritional yeast, and serve.

HERB WELLNESS BOWL

SERVES: 4

Prep Time: 15 minutes **Cook Time:** n/a

ALMOND DRESSING

1 teaspoon finely chopped tarragon leaves
1 teaspoon Dijon mustard
Zest and juice of 1 large lemon
3 tablespoons extra-virgin olive oil
½ cup (70 g) almonds, toasted and chopped
Sea salt and freshly ground black pepper

1 handful dill fronds
1 handful flat-leaf parsley leaves
1 handful coriander leaves
1 handful chervil leaves
1 handful basil leaves
1 handful mint leaves
1 handful chives, snipped
4¼ cups (300 g) shredded savoy cabbage

1. To make the dressing, place the tarragon, mustard, and lemon zest and juice in a small bowl and whisk. Slowly whisk in the olive oil until well combined, then stir in the almonds. Season with salt and pepper.
2. To assemble the salad, place the herbs and cabbage in a large bowl. Drizzle on the dressing and gently toss to coat. Season with more salt and pepper, if needed.

Note:

You could replace the lemon zest and juice in the dressing with 2 tablespoons of vinegar: try apple cider vinegar or white or red wine vinegar.

GARLICKY BRAISED GREENS

SERVES: 4

Prep Time: 10 minutes **Cook Time:** 12–15 minutes

2 cups (480) ml Chicken Bone Broth (page 239)
6 Swiss chard, leaves and stems separated and cut into 3-inch (8-cm) lengths
½ bunch of kale (about 5 ounces / 150 g), stems discarded and leaves torn
1 bunch of English spinach (about 7 ounces / 200 g), stems removed
Sea salt and freshly ground black pepper
⅓ cup (80 ml) good-quality animal fat
5 cloves garlic, thinly sliced
2 teaspoons lemon juice

1. Pour the chicken broth into a large saucepan and bring to a simmer over medium heat. Add the Swiss chard stems, reduce the heat to medium–low, and simmer for 5 minutes. Next, add the kale, Swiss chard leaves, and spinach, cover with a lid, and cook for 5–6 minutes until the leaves are wilted. Season with salt and pepper.
2. Meanwhile, in a skillet over medium heat, gently heat the fat, then add the garlic and cook for about 1–2 minutes, or until it just starts to color. Remove from the heat, add the lemon juice and stir through.
3. When the greens are ready, pour the garlic dressing on top, season with some more salt and pepper, if needed, and serve immediately.

WHOLE ROASTED CAULIFLOWER WITH ALMONDS AND DUKKAH

SERVES: 4–6

Prep Time: 20 minutes **Cook Time:** 1 hour 10 minutes–1 hour 40 minutes

- 1 large head cauliflower (about 2 pounds/ 900 g)
- 3 tablespoons coconut oil or good-quality animal fat
- 2 yellow onions, finely chopped
- 5 cloves garlic, finely sliced
- 1½ teaspoons ground turmeric
- 2 teaspoons cumin seeds
- 1 (14-ounce/400-g) can diced tomatoes (or 400 g tomatoes, diced)
- 2 pinches saffron
- 2 cups (480 ml) Beef or Chicken Bone Broth (pages 238 and 239) or water
- Sea salt and freshly ground black pepper
- 1 cup (140 g) almonds (activated if possible), toasted and chopped
- 1 cup (120 g) dukkah
- ½ bunch of kale, silverbeet, or spinach (about 7 ounces / 200 g), stalks removed, leaves torn (reserve the stalks for broths)

1. Preheat the oven to 350°F (180°C).
2. Remove the leaves and cut away the stalk from the base of the cauliflower.
3. Melt the oil or fat in a large flameproof casserole dish that will fit your whole cauliflower. Add the onion and cook over medium heat for 5 minutes until soft.
4. Stir in the garlic and cook for 1 minute, then add the turmeric and cumin seeds and cook for 30 seconds until fragrant.
5. Add the tomatoes, saffron, and broth or water to the dish, stir and bring to a boil. Remove from the heat and season with salt and pepper.
6. Place the cauliflower in the dish and spoon the sauce over the top. Cover with foil and roast, basting every 20 minutes with the sauce, for 1–1½ hours until tender. Add a little more broth or water if it starts to look dry. Remove from the oven and set aside to cool a little.
7. Combine the almonds and dukkah and mix well.
8. When the cauliflower is cool enough to touch, coat it with the dukkah mixture, pressing it in with your hands to form an even crust. Scatter the kale over the sauce and mix through. Return to the oven and roast, uncovered, for a further 8–10 minutes until the cauliflower crust is golden brown.

SPICED BUTTERNUT SQUASH SOUP

SERVES: 6

Prep Time: 15–20 minutes **Cook Time:** 40 minutes

- **3 tablespoons coconut oil or good-quality animal fat**
- **2¼-pound (1-kg) butternut squash (or any other pumpkin variety), peeled and diced**
- **1 carrot, diced**
- **1 large yellow onion, finely chopped**
- **4 cloves garlic, crushed**
- **5½ cups (1.3 liters) Chicken Bone Broth (page 239) or vegetable stock**
- **1½ tablespoons finely grated ginger**
- **1½ tablespoons ras el hanout**
- **1½ teaspoons ground cumin**
- **6 saffron threads**
- **1 cup (240 ml) coconut cream, plus extra to serve**
- **Sea salt and freshly ground black pepper**
- **Cilantro and mint leaves, to serve**
- **Chili powder, to serve**

1. Melt the oil or fat in a large saucepan over medium heat. Add the butternut squash, carrot, onion, and garlic and sauté, stirring occasionally, for about 10 minutes, until the onion is translucent.
2. Add the broth or stock, ginger, ras el hanout, cumin, and saffron.
3. Reduce the heat, cover and simmer, stirring occasionally, for about 30 minutes, or until the carrot and butternut squash are tender.
4. Add the coconut cream and puree the soup using a handheld blender. Season with salt and pepper.
5. Ladle the soup into bowls, drizzle with a little extra coconut cream, and top with some cilantro and mint leaves and chili powder.

GREEK-STYLE BROCCOLI SALAD

SERVES: 2–4 AS A SIDE

Prep Time: 15 minutes (plus 30 minutes to marinate) **Cook Time:** 1 minute

PICKLED RED ONION

½ red onion, cut into 8 wedges
⅓ cup (80 ml) red wine vinegar
1 teaspoon honey

DRESSING

⅓ cup plus 1 tablespoon (100 ml) extra-virgin olive oil
1 tablespoon lemon juice
1 clove garlic, finely grated
½ teaspoon Dijon mustard
1 teaspoon dried oregano

Sea salt and freshly ground black pepper
1 large head broccoli (about 14 ounces/400 g), cut into bite-sized florets
¾ cup (120 g) semi-dried tomatoes (to make your own see page 284)
⅔ cup (100 g) pitted kalamata olives, halved
2 tablespoons sliced almonds, toasted
1 large handful basil leaves

1. Place the pickled red onion ingredients in a small saucepan and bring to a simmer over medium heat. Cover with a lid and cook for 1 minute, then remove from the heat and allow to cool completely. Drain, reserving 2 tablespoons of the pickling vinegar for the dressing (save the rest for another use).
2. Combine all the dressing ingredients in a bowl and season to taste with salt and pepper. Add the reserved pickling vinegar and mix well.
3. Place the broccoli in a large bowl, pour over half the dressing, and toss until the broccoli is well coated. Set aside to marinate for 30 minutes to allow the broccoli to soften slightly and become more flavorsome.
4. Add the pickled red onion, semi-dried tomatoes, olives, almonds, and basil to the marinated broccoli and gently toss. Season with salt and pepper if needed. Arrange on a large platter, drizzle over some more dressing, and serve.

HASSELBACK SWEET POTATOES WITH SALMORIGLIO

SERVES: 4 AS A SIDE

Prep Time: 15 minutes **Cook Time:** 1 hour and 20 minutes (or more, depending on the size)

4 sweet potatoes
2 tablespoons coconut oil or good-quality animal fat, melted
2 tablespoons olive oil
2 teaspoons finely chopped thyme leaves
4 cloves garlic, finely grated
Sea salt and freshly ground black pepper

SALMORIGLIO

3 cloves garlic, peeled
1 handful oregano leaves
1 large handful flat-leaf parsley leaves
½ cup (120 ml) extra-virgin olive oil
Juice of 1 lemon

1. Preheat the oven to 400°F (200°C) or 355°F (180°C fan-forced/convection). Line a baking sheet with parchment paper.
2. Without cutting all the way through and stopping about ½ inch (1 cm) from the base, cut across each sweet potato at ¼ inch (5 mm) intervals. (You can use two chopsticks to help here: place a chopstick along each long side of the sweet potato and then slice; the chopsticks stop you from cutting all the way through.) Carefully transfer the sliced sweet potatoes to the prepared tray.
3. Combine the coconut oil or fat, olive oil, thyme, and garlic in a small bowl and season with salt and pepper.
4. Rub the garlic and thyme oil all over the sweet potatoes, getting it in between the slices, and bake for about 1 hour 20 minutes, or until the sweet potatoes are crispy on top and tender in the middle. (All sweet potatoes are different sizes so you may need a little longer.)
5. Meanwhile, to make the salmoriglio, pound the garlic and a pinch of salt to a paste using a mortar and pestle (or you can use a handheld blender or food processor). Add the oregano and parsley, again pound to a paste, then stir in the olive oil and lemon juice. Season to taste with salt.
6. Sprinkle the hasselback sweet potatoes with extra salt, if desired, spoon over the salmoriglio and serve.

CABBAGE ROASTED IN DUCK FAT

SERVES: 4 AS A SIDE

Prep Time: 5–8 minutes **Cook Time:** 23 minutes

GARLIC SALT

1 teaspoon garlic powder
1½ teaspoons fennel seeds, crushed using a mortar and pestle
½ teaspoon freshly ground black pepper
3 teaspoons sea salt

⅓ cup (80 ml) melted duck fat or coconut oil
1 small green or savoy cabbage, cut into ¾-inch (2-cm) thick slices
1 cup (240 ml) Chicken Bone Broth (page 239)

1. Place all the garlic salt ingredients in a small bowl and mix to combine.
2. Preheat the oven to 400°F (200°C) or 355°F (180°C fan-forced/convection).
3. Heat a grill pan over medium–high heat. Brush the grill with some of the duck fat or coconut oil and grill the cabbage on both sides for 2–2½ minutes, or until charred.
4. Transfer the cabbage to a roasting pan and spread out to form a single layer. Drizzle over the remaining duck fat or coconut oil and season with a big pinch of garlic salt. Pour in the broth and roast for 17–20 minutes, or until the cabbage is cooked through.
5. To serve, place the roasted cabbage slices on a large platter, pour on the juices from the roasting pan, and season with more garlic salt if needed.

Tip:

Store the leftover garlic salt in an airtight container in the pantry for up to 3 months.

MOROCCAN CARROT SALAD

SERVES: 4

Prep Time: 15 minutes **Cook Time:** n/a

- 4 tablespoons extra-virgin olive oil
- 1 tablespoon lemon juice
- 1 tablespoon apple cider vinegar
- 1 tablespoon honey
- 1 teaspoon grated fresh ginger
- 1 long red chili, deseeded and finely chopped, *optional*
- ½ teaspoon ground sumac
- 4 large carrots, grated
- 1 handful almonds (activated if possible, see page 274), toasted and chopped
- 1 large handful chopped cilantro leaves
- 1 handful chopped mint leaves
- 3 tablespoons dried currants
- Sea salt and freshly ground black pepper

1. In a large serving bowl, whisk together the olive oil, lemon juice, vinegar, honey, and ginger until well combined. Add the chili, sumac, carrot, almonds, coriander, mint, and barberries or currants. Toss; season with salt and pepper.
2. Serve alongside your favorite protein or as part of a spread of salads at a barbecue.

VEGETABLE MASALA

SERVES: 4

Prep Time: 25–30 minutes **Cook Time:** 50 minutes

SPICE MIX

1 cinnamon stick
8 cloves
8 cardamom pods, crushed
1 teaspoon fennel seeds
2 teaspoons cumin seeds
2 teaspoons coriander seeds
1 teaspoon ground turmeric
½ teaspoon chili powder

2 tablespoons coconut oil
1 yellow onion, chopped
3 cloves garlic, finely chopped
8 curry leaves, chopped
1 long green chili, halved, deseeded and thinly sliced
1 tablespoon finely grated ginger
1½ tablespoons finely chopped cilantro leaves
2 cups (480 ml) coconut cream
1 tablespoon poppy seeds
½ cup (50 g) cashew nuts (activated if possible, see page 274), chopped
14 ounces (400 g) diced tomatoes
½ cup (120 ml) Chicken Bone Broth (page 239) or water
1 carrot, diced
1 zucchini, diced
3½ ounces (100 g) green beans, cut into 1½-inch (4-cm) batons
3½ ounces (100 g) broccoli florets

1. To make the spice mix, toast the whole spices and seeds until fragrant, then grind in a spice grinder or with a mortar and pestle. Mix through the turmeric and chili powder. Set aside until needed.
2. Melt the oil in a large saucepan over medium heat. Add the onion and cook for 5 minutes, or until softened. Stir in the garlic, spice mix, and curry leaves and cook for about 30 seconds, or until fragrant. Add the chili, ginger, and chopped cilantro and cook for 1 minute to soften, then stir in the coconut cream, poppy seeds, cashews, tomatoes, and chicken broth or water. Mix well and bring to a simmer, then reduce the heat to low, cover with a lid, and cook for 20 minutes to allow the flavors to develop.
3. Add the carrot and cook for 10 minutes, then add the remaining vegetables, cover, and cook for a further 20 minutes, or until all the vegetables are tender. Season with salt and pepper.
4. Sprinkle the cilantro leaves over the vegetable masala and serve with the cauliflower rice and a wedge or two of lemon to squeeze on top.

3½ ounces (100 g) eggplant, cut into ½-inch (1.5-cm) dice
3½ ounces (100 g) kabocha squash, cut into ½-inch (1.5-cm) dice
Sea salt and freshly ground black pepper

TO SERVE

Cilantro leaves
Cooked Cauliflower Rice (page 286)
Lemon wedges

MAHA HEALTHY DRINKS: SIP THE GOOD LIFE

Welcome to MAHA's refreshing world of healthy drinks, where every sip bursts with vitality. Imagine vibrant smoothies packed with goodness, zesty ginger-infused tonics, or warming herbal teas that soothe and energize. This chapter is your guide to crafting beverages that nourish and delight, using fresh, wholesome ingredients that keep things simple and budget friendly. These recipes elevate hydration into an art form. Grab your blender or kettle, toss in some vibrant produce, and let's mix up drinks that make every moment feel invigorating and joyful.

CHAI-SPICED ROOIBOS TEA

SERVES: 1

Prep Time: 5 minutes **Cook Time:** 5 minutes

2 cinnamon sticks
1½ teaspoons cardamom pods
1 teaspoon cloves
¾ cup (40 g) loose rooibos tea leaves
1 teaspoon black peppercorns
1 teaspoon Chinese five spice
1½ cups (375 ml) plant-based milk of your choice (such as almond or coconut)
1 teaspoon finely grated ginger
Sweetener of your choice (liquid stevia, xylitol, monk fruit sweetener, honey), to taste

1. To make the chai-spiced rooibos tea, break the cinnamon sticks into small shards and place in a mortar. Add the cardamom pods and cloves and pound with a pestle until coarsely ground (or use a spice grinder). Transfer to a bowl, add the rooibos tea leaves, peppercorns, and five spice and mix well.
2. Pour the milk into a small saucepan and mix in the ginger and 3 teaspoons of chai-spiced rooibos tea. Cover with a lid and warm over medium–low heat for 5 minutes. Don't let the milk boil.
3. Remove the pan from the heat and let steep, covered, for about 10 minutes to allow the flavors to infuse. If needed, reheat to the desired temperature—again, don't allow the milk to boil.
4. Strain the tea into a mug or glass, sweeten with your sweetener of choice, and enjoy!

Tip:

Transfer the remaining chai-spiced rooibos tea to an airtight container and store in the pantry for up to 3 months.

TURMERIC AND GINGER ELIXIR

MAKES: 2 CUPS (480 ML)

Prep Time: 5 minutes (plus 1 hour to steep) **Cook Time:** n/a

17½ ounces (500 g) fresh turmeric
10½ ounces (300 g) ginger
2½ tablespoons filtered water
2 teaspoons monk fruit sweetener or manuka honey, or to taste
¼ teaspoon ground cinnamon
Pinch freshly ground black pepper

1. You'll need a ½-quart (500 ml) preserving jar with a lid for this recipe. Wash the jar in very hot water or run it through a hot rinse cycle in the dishwasher.
2. Juice the turmeric and ginger in a cold press juicer. Mix in the water, sweetener, cinnamon, and pepper and pour into the sterilized jar. Cover and allow to steep for 1 hour before drinking.
3. Take a 2 tablespoon (30 ml) dose up to three times a day. Store the turmeric elixir in the fridge for up to 5 days.

PETE'S COLD AND FLU TONIC

SERVES: 4–6

Prep Time: 5 minutes **Cook Time:** about 1 hour

4 garlic bulbs
2-inch (5-cm) piece of ginger
3 lemons
Manuka honey, to taste, *optional*

1. Roughly chop the garlic, ginger, and lemons. Place in a large saucepan and cover with 2 quarts (2 liters) of water. Bring to a boil, then reduce the heat to low and simmer for 1 hour.
2. Strain the tonic into a jug, add the manuka honey to taste, and drink up to four glasses per day. Store in an airtight glass bottle in the fridge for up to 1 week

HOT CHOCOLATE WITH COLLAGEN

SERVES: 1

Prep Time: 1- 2 minutes **Cook Time:** 1–2 minutes

1¼ cups (300 ml) coconut milk (you can also use almond, macadamia, or hemp milk)

1–2 tablespoons chocolate collagen blend

Sweetener of your choice (liquid stevia, xylitol, monk fruit sweetener, honey), to taste, *optional*

Pour the milk into a small saucepan. Stir through the collagen blend to combine. Heat over medium–low heat, stirring occasionally, until heated through. Pour into a mug, sip, and enjoy!

MAHA HEALTHY TREATS AND DESSERTS: SWEET BLISS, GUILT-FREE

Enjoy MAHA's sweet escape, where healthy treats and desserts spark joy without the guilt. Recipes include decadent chocolate mud cake, crunchy maple kissed cookies, or fresh fruit coconut jellies bursting with color. This chapter transforms wholesome ingredients into indulgent delights that keep your budget in check. From creamy and refreshing avocado, mint, and chocolate ice pops on a hot summer's day, to blushing ripe strawberries simply dipped in chocolate, every recipe is a celebration of flavor and feel-good vibes. Whether you're enjoying a quick snack or a showstopping finale, these sweets deliver. Grab your mixing bowl, let your kitchen hum with sweetness, and whip up treats that make every moment deliciously wholesome.

JAFFA TRUFFLES

MAKES: APPROX. 50 SMALL TRUFFLES (DEPENDING ON SIZE)

Prep Time: 30 minutes (plus chilling)

1¼ cups (300 g) coconut oil or ghee
¾ cup (200 g) coconut butter
2 tablespoons coconut cream
3 tablespoons manuka honey (or liquid stevia, to taste)
4 cups (1 pound 5 ounces / 600 g) chopped dark (70–90% cacao) chocolate, *divided*
4–5 drops of essential orange oil
Cacao powder, for dusting

Note:

You'll need to start these a day ahead.

1. Line a large baking sheet with parchment paper.
2. Place the coconut oil or ghee, coconut butter, coconut cream, and honey in the bowl of an stand mixer fitted with the paddle attachment. Mix, scraping down the side of the bowl from time to time, until pale and creamy.
3. Meanwhile, melt half the chocolate in a heatproof bowl over a saucepan of just-simmering water. (Make sure the bowl doesn't touch the water or it will overheat and the chocolate will seize.) Stir in the orange oil with a metal spoon. Leave to cool until still runny but not hot.
4. With the motor still running, slowly pour the melted chocolate into the coconut oil or ghee mixture and mix until combined and a little fluffy. (If it becomes soft and runny, simply pop it in the fridge for 30–50 minutes, or until cool and slightly firm, then mix again using the stand mixer until whipped and fluffy.)
5. Spoon the chocolate mixture into a piping bag fitted with a ⅓-inch (8-mm) straight-edge nozzle. Pipe ½-inch (1-cm) chocolate teardrop shapes onto the prepared tray, then place in the fridge for 1 hour, or until firm.
6. Melt the remaining chocolate, then cool slightly. Using a fork, dip the chocolate teardrops into the melted chocolate, gently shake to remove the excess, return to the tray, and dust with the cacao powder. Refrigerate, uncovered, overnight to set.
7. Place the jaffa truffles on a platter and serve. Store the truffles in an airtight container in the fridge for up to 3 weeks.

STRAWBERRY AND COCONUT CREAMS

MAKES: 40–45

1 cup (150 g) frozen strawberries, thawed
¼ teaspoon liquid stevia (or 2 teaspoons xylitol or honey)
1 tablespoon powdered gelatin

COCONUT CREAM LAYER

1 cup (120 ml) coconut cream
¼ teaspoon liquid stevia (or 2 teaspoons xylitol or honey)
1 tablespoon powdered gelatin

1. Combine the strawberries and 3 tablespoons of water in a blender and pulse a couple of times to form a puree. Strain through a fine sieve into a small saucepan. (Discard the leftover strawberry pulp.) Stir in the stevia, sprinkle over the gelatin, and stir until the gelatin is incorporated. Allow to stand for 5 minutes.
2. Place the pan over medium–low heat and cook, stirring constantly, for 5 minutes until the strawberry mixture is completely smooth. Make sure you don't boil the mixture.
3. Pour the strawberry mixture into silicon ice-cube trays or chocolate molds until half full, then immediately place in the freezer for 15 minutes to set.
4. Meanwhile, to make the coconut cream layer, place the coconut cream and stevia in a small saucepan and stir to combine. Sprinkle the powdered gelatin over 2 tablespoons of water and allow to stand for 5 minutes to bloom, then stir the gelatin through the hot coconut cream mixture to combine. Cook, stirring constantly, over medium–low heat for 5 minutes until completely smooth. Do not allow the mixture to boil. Set aside to cool to lukewarm.
5. Once the strawberry jellies have set, pour the cooled coconut mixture into the ice-cube tray or chocolate molds until filled to the top and immediately place in the freezer for a further 15 minutes until set.
6. Remove the jellies from the molds and store in an airtight jar. They will keep for a few weeks in the fridge.

CHOCOLATE MUD CAKE

SERVES: 6–8

Prep Time: 25 minutes **Cook Time:** 40 minutes (plus 4 hours chilling time)

- **2 cups (10½ ounces / 300 g) finely chopped dark (85–90% cacao) chocolate**
- **¾ cup plus 1 tablespoon (200 ml) melted coconut oil or ghee**
- **6 organic, free-range eggs, separated**
- **1 cup (180 g) finely ground monk fruit sweetener, *divided***
- **1½ cups (150 g) almond meal**
- **2 teaspoons baking powder**
- **Pinch sea salt**
- **¾ cup (90 g) raspberries**
- **Raspberry and Chia Sauce (page 283), to serve**

CHOCOLATE GANACHE

- **1 cup (150 g) finely chopped dark (85–90% cacao) chocolate**
- **⅔ cup (150 ml) coconut cream, plus extra if needed**

1. Preheat the oven to 320°F (160°C) or 285°F (140°C convection/fan-forced). Grease a 10-inch (25-cm) round cake pan and line the base and sides with parchment paper.
2. Combine the chocolate and coconut oil or ghee in a heatproof bowl and place over a saucepan of just-simmering water. Stir occasionally with a metal spoon until melted and smooth. (Make sure the bowl doesn't touch the water or it will overheat and the chocolate will seize.)
3. Meanwhile, place the egg yolks and half the monk fruit sweetener in the bowl of an electric mixer and mix on medium–high speed using the whisk attachment until the mixture is doubled in size and fluffy. Fold into the melted chocolate mixture until incorporated. Sift in the almond meal, baking powder, and salt and fold through.
4. Clean the bowl and whisk attachment. Add the egg whites and the remaining monk fruit sweetener to the bowl and whisk until soft peaks form.
5. Gently fold the egg white mixture into the chocolate mixture. Pour into the prepared tin and smooth the top with a spatula. Bake for 40 minutes, or until the cake has risen a little and is cooked through. (The cake is cooked when a skewer inserted in the center comes out clean.) Allow to cool completely in the pan, then place in the refrigerator for 4 hours to chill.

6. **To make the chocolate ganache:** Place the chocolate in a heatproof bowl and set aside. Pour the coconut cream into a small saucepan and bring to a boil over low heat. Remove from the heat and slowly pour over the chocolate, stirring constantly with a metal spoon, until the chocolate has melted and the ganache is smooth and shiny. If the ganache looks like it is splitting, add a dash of extra coconut cream and mix to incorporate.
7. Turn the chilled cake out onto a platter and spread the chocolate ganache over the top. Scatter over the raspberries and drizzle over the raspberry and chia sauce.

NIC'S CAMU CAMU SLAB

SERVES: 6–8

Prep Time: 10–15 minutes (plus 2 hours to set)

⅓ cup plus 1 tablespoon (100 ml) melted coconut oil
½ cup (120 ml) melted cacao butter
3 tablespoons cacao powder
3 tablespoons carob powder
1 teaspoon camu camu berry powder
¼ cup (80 g) honey
1 teaspoon ground cinnamon
1¾ cup (250 g) macadamia nuts (activated if possible, see page 274), toasted and roughly chopped
Pinch sea salt

1. Line a 10 × 6-inch (26 cm × 16 cm) tray with plastic wrap.
2. Place all the ingredients in a bowl and stir well. Spread out on the prepared tray and place in the fridge for 2 hours, or until set. (If you are in a hurry, pop the slab in the freezer and it will set even faster.)
3. Turn out the slab onto a chopping board and chop or break into bite-sized pieces.

TIP:

You will need to store the chocolate in an airtight container in the fridge, as it will melt at room temperature. The chocolate will keep for 2–3 weeks, but if your family is like mine, it won't last nearly that long.

COUGH DROP GUMMIES

MAKES: 40

Prep Time: 15–20 minutes (plus 1 hour to infuse and 15 minutes to set)
Cook Time: 3 minutes

- **1½ cups (360 ml) filtered water, *divided***
- **2 lemongrass stems, pale part only, bruised with the back of a knife**
- **2-inch (5-cm) piece of ginger, chopped**
- **½ teaspoon ground turmeric**
- **Pinch ground cloves**
- **5 tablespoons (50 g) powdered gelatin**
- **3 tablespoons lemon juice**
- **3 tablespoons honey (we use manuka honey)**

1. Place 3/4 cup (180 ml) of the filtered water and the lemongrass, ginger, turmeric, and cloves in a small saucepan. Stir and bring to a boil over medium heat. Turn off the heat, cover with the lid, and allow to stand for 1 hour so the flavors infuse.
2. Meanwhile, sprinkle the gelatin over the remaining 3/4 cup (180 ml) of water, mix well and allow to stand for at least 5 minutes for the gelatin granules to expand and soften.
3. Bring the lemongrass and ginger–infused water to a simmer over medium–low heat, stir through the gelatin mixture, and continue to stir for 3 minutes, or until the gelatin has completely dissolved. Remove from the heat, then stir in the lemon juice and honey and mix until the honey dissolves.
4. Pass the liquid through a fine strainer, discard the lemongrass and ginger, then pour into a silicone ice-cube tray or mini silicone molds. Transfer to the freezer for 15 minutes, or until set.
5. Remove the gummies from the molds and store in the fridge in an airtight container for up to 2 weeks.

CHOCOLATE, MINT, AND AVOCADO ICE POPS

MAKES: 8

Prep Time: 10 minutes **Freeze Time:** 6–8 hours total

½ avocado
4 fresh medjool dates, pitted
3 tablespoons cacao powder
1½ cups (350 ml) Whipped Coconut Cream (page 282)
⅔ cup (150 ml) Beef Bone Broth (page 238)
4–6 drops of edible peppermint oil, or to taste
1 tablespoon honey

1. Combine all the ingredients in a high-speed blender and blend until smooth.
2. Pour the mixture into popsicle molds and freeze for 2 hours.
3. Insert a popsicle stick in the middle of each mold, then return to the freezer for 4–6 hours until frozen.
4. Serve.

COCONUT PANNA COTTA WITH RED WINE POACHED PEARS, CHERRIES & PISTACHIO

SERVES: 4

Prep Time: 20 minutes **Cook Time:** 25 minutes (4–6 hours chilling time)

PANNA COTTA

2 cups (500 ml) coconut cream
¼ cup (60 ml) honey
1 vanilla bean, split lengthways, seeds scraped
1½ teaspoons grass-fed gelatin powder
3 tablespoons coconut milk

RED WINE POACHED PEARS

1 cup (240 ml) red wine
2 cups (500 ml) water
Zest and juice of 1 lemon
½ cup (120 ml) honey
½ vanilla bean, split
1 cinnamon stick
5 whole cloves
2 small ripe pears, peeled and halved, core removed

TO SERVE

Fresh cherries
Toasted pistachios, roughly chopped

1. **To make the panna cotta:** In a saucepan over medium heat, combine the coconut cream, honey, and vanilla bean (pod and seeds). Stir until the honey is dissolved and the mixture just comes to a boil. Remove from heat.
2. In a small bowl, mix the gelatin powder into the coconut milk and let bloom for 2 minutes.
3. Whisk the gelatin mixture into the hot cream until fully dissolved.
4. Strain the mixture through a fine sieve and divide between 4 dessert bowls or glasses.
5. Refrigerate for 4–6 hours, or until fully set.
6. **To poach the pears:** In a medium saucepan, combine the red wine, water, lemon juice and zest, honey, vanilla, cinnamon stick, and cloves. Bring to a simmer.
7. Add the pear halves and cook gently, turning occasionally, for about 25 minutes or until tender when pierced with a knife.
8. Remove pears and let them cool in the syrup. Once cool, reduce the syrup over medium heat for 10–15 minutes until slightly thickened.
9. Once the panna cotta is set, top each serving with a poached pear half, a few fresh cherries, a drizzle of red wine syrup, and a generous sprinkle of chopped toasted pistachios. Serve chilled.

BURNT ORANGE CRÈME CATALANE

SERVES: 4

Prep Time: 15 minutes **Cook Time:** 30 minutes (plus 2–4 hours chilling time)

Zest of 2 oranges
3⅓ cups (800 ml) coconut cream
1 vanilla bean, split (or 1 teaspoon vanilla paste)
8 egg yolks
½ cup honey
2 teaspoons powdered gelatin
3 tablespoons cold water, for blooming gelatin
4 teaspoons coconut sugar, for brûlée topping

TO SERVE

Fresh orange slices or segments
Cacao nibs
Dark chocolate shavings

1. Combine the coconut cream, orange zest, and split vanilla bean in a small saucepan. Bring to a gentle simmer over medium heat, stirring occasionally. Remove from the heat and let it steep for 5 minutes.
2. In a separate bowl, whisk together the egg yolks and honey until smooth. Gradually pour in half of the warm cream mixture while whisking constantly, then add the remaining cream and whisk until fully combined.
3. Pour the custard into a deep baking dish. Bake at 350°F (180°C) for 25–30 minutes, or until the surface is caramelized and the center has a gentle wobble.
4. While the custard bakes, sprinkle the gelatin over the cold water and let bloom for 5–10 minutes. Once the custard is out of the oven and still warm, stir in the bloomed gelatin until fully dissolved. The custard will look like scrambled eggs at this point.
5. Remove the vanilla bean and scrape out the seeds. Blend the custard until smooth, then strain through a fine mesh sieve.
6. Pour the custard into clean ramekins or serving bowls. Refrigerate for 2–4 hours, or until fully set.
7. Just before serving, sprinkle each custard with 1 teaspoon of coconut sugar. Use a kitchen torch to caramelize the sugar until golden and crisp.
8. Garnish with fresh orange slices, cacao nibs, and dark chocolate shavings.

PECAN PIE

SERVES 8–12

Prep Time: 35–45 minutes **Cooking time:** 45–50 minutes

SWEET PASTRY CRUST

1 Sweet Pastry—see recipe on page 236 (chill before use)

PECAN FILLING

- **1 pound (450 g) pitted Medjool dates, soaked in warm water for 20 minutes then drained**
- **⅔ cup (200 ml) good-quality maple syrup, plus extra to serve if desired**
- **½ cup (125 ml) melted coconut oil**
- **6 organic, free-range eggs**
- **1 teaspoon vanilla extract**
- **1 teaspoon sea salt**
- **2 cups (240 g) chopped pecans (for the filling)**
- **1 cup (100 g) whole pecans (for the top)**

1. **To prepare the pastry crust:** Preheat the oven to 320°F (160°C fan-forced/convection).
2. Grease a 14 × 4-inch (35 × 13-cm) rectangular tart tin, or a 9-inch (23-cm) round tart tin, with coconut oil.
3. Remove the chilled pastry from the refrigerator and unwrap.
4. Lightly dust a large sheet of parchment paper with arrowroot flour and place the dough on top. Lay another large sheet of parchment paper over the dough and roll it out evenly between the sheets to a thickness of ⅛ inch (3 mm) and large enough to cover the tin.
5. Peel off the top sheet, place the tart tin upside down on the exposed pastry, and flip the whole thing over. Gently press the dough into the tin, then peel off the remaining parchment paper.
6. Press the pastry into the corners and up the sides of the tin. If the pastry tears, patch it with extra pieces and press to seal.
7. Trim the edges and prick the base with a fork to prevent air bubbles.
8. **To make the pecan filling:** In a food processor, combine the dates, maple syrup, coconut oil, eggs, vanilla, and salt. Blend until smooth and well combined.
9. Stir in the chopped pecans or pulse briefly to incorporate.
10. **To assemble and bake:** Pour the filling into the prepared tart shell and sprinkle the whole pecans on top.
11. Bake for 45–50 minutes, or until the tart is set and a skewer inserted in the center comes out clean. If the crust edges begin to brown too quickly, cover them with foil partway through baking.
12. Allow to cool completely before slicing. Optional: Drizzle with a little extra maple syrup before serving.

SWEET PASTRY

MAKES: 12 OUNCES (350 G)

Prep Time: 15 minutes (plus 30 minutes to firm up before rolling)

1 cup (100 g) almond meal
⅓ cup (50 g) coconut flour
¼ cup (30 g) arrowroot
3¾ ounces (½ cup / 105 g) ghee or coconut oil, cold
3 tablespoons honey
1 organic, free-range egg

Note:

Making dough without gluten can be challenging because gluten helps bind baked goods, giving the dough elasticity. This dough is not like your regular dough and it may crack easily when rolled and lining the tarts.

1. In a mixing bowl, add the almond meal, coconut flour, and arrowroot. Mix to combine.
2. Cut the ghee or coconut oil into small pieces and work the ghee or coconut oil into the dry mix using your hands to form fine crumbs.
3. Add the honey and mix until it forms a ball of dough. Transfer the dough onto a working bench dusted with arrowroot and knead the dough until smooth (don't be alarmed if the dough appears to be slightly moist or sticky). Wrap the dough with plastic wrap and refrigerate for 30 minutes or until it is firm enough to roll out.
4. The dough can be stored refrigerated for up to 1 week and in the freezer for up to 3 months.

Note:

This recipe can also be used as a savory pastry. Just omit the honey and add a few pinches of sea salt to make a savoury crust/pastry—perfect for pies and quiches.

MAHA ESSENTIALS

MAHA BONE BROTHS: SOUL-WARMING ELIXIRS

Sip into MAHA's bone broths, where simple ingredients become nourishing magic. Picture slow-simmered pots yielding rich, savory broths packed with warmth and goodness. This chapter celebrates budget-friendly bones transformed into golden elixirs, perfect for sipping or enhancing dishes. From classic beef to fragrant chicken broth, each recipe is a cozy hug in a mug. Grab your stockpot, let the kitchen fill with comforting aromas, and craft broths that soothe the soul.

BEEF BONE BROTH

MAKES: 4¼ QUARTS (4 LITERS)

Prep Time: 15 minutes (plus 1 hour standing time) **Cook Time:** 6–12 hours

- About 4⅓ pounds (2 kg) beef knuckle and marrow bones
- 1 calf foot, chopped into pieces, *optional*
- 3 tablespoons apple cider vinegar
- 3⅓ pounds (1.5 kg) meaty beef rib or neck bones
- 3 onions, roughly chopped
- 3 carrots, roughly chopped
- 3 celery stalks, roughly chopped
- 2 leeks, white part only, roughly chopped
- 3 thyme sprigs
- 2 bay leaves
- 1 teaspoon black peppercorns, crushed
- 1 garlic bulb, cut in half horizontally
- 2 large handfuls flat-leaf parsley stalks

1. Place the knuckle and marrow bones and calf foot (if using) in a stockpot, add the vinegar, and pour in 5¼ quarts (5 liters) of cold water, or enough to cover. Set aside for 1 hour to help draw out the nutrients from the bones. Remove the bones from the water, reserving the water.
2. Preheat the oven to 350°F (180°C).
3. Place the knuckle and marrow bones, calf foot (if using), and meaty bones in a few large roasting pans and roast in the oven for 30–40 minutes until well browned. Return all the bones to the pot and add the vegetables.
4. Pour the fat from the roasting pans into a saucepan, add 1 quart (1 liter) of the reserved water, place over high heat and bring to a simmer, stirring with a wooden spoon to loosen any coagulated juices. Add this liquid to the bones and vegetables. If necessary, add the remaining reserved water to the pot to just cover the bones—the liquid should come no higher than ¾-inch (2-cm) below the rim of the pot, as the volume will increase slightly during cooking.
5. Bring the broth to a boil, skimming off the scum that rises to the top.
6. Reduce the heat to low and add the thyme, bay leaves, peppercorns, and garlic. Simmer for 12–24 hours. Just before finishing, add the parsley and simmer for 10 minutes. Strain the broth into a large container, cover, and place in the fridge overnight. Remove the congealed fat that rises to the top and reserve for cooking; it will keep in the fridge for up to 1 week or in the freezer for up to 3 months.
7. Transfer the thick and gelatinous broth to smaller airtight containers and place in the fridge or, for long-term storage, the freezer. The broth can be stored in the fridge for 3–4 days or frozen for up to 3 months.

CHICKEN BONE BROTH

MAKES: 4 QUARTS (4 LITERS)

Prep Time: 15 minutes **Cooking time:** 6–12 hours

5½ pounds (2.5 kg) bony chicken parts (such as necks, breastbones, and wings)
2–4 chicken feet
2 tablespoons apple cider vinegar
1 large yellow onion, roughly chopped
2 carrots, roughly chopped
3 celery stalks, roughly chopped
1 leek, white part only, rinsed and roughly chopped
1 garlic bulb, broken into cloves
1 tablespoon black peppercorns, lightly crushed
2 large handfuls flat-leaf parsley, leaves and stalks
2 bay leaves

1. Place the chicken pieces in a stockpot or very large saucepan. Add 5 quarts (5 liters) of cold water, the vinegar, onion, carrot, celery, leek, garlic, and peppercorns.
2. Place the stockpot or pan over medium–high heat and bring to a boil, skimming off the scum that forms on the surface. Reduce the heat to low and simmer for 6–12 hours. The longer you cook the broth the more the flavor develops.
3. Allow the broth to cool slightly, then strain through a fine sieve into a large storage container. Cover and place in the fridge until the fat rises to the top and congeals.
4. Skim off this layer of fat (it is a fantastic, stable cooking fat) and store it in a glass storage container in the fridge for up to 2 weeks—use it for frying and sautéing.
5. Transfer the broth to smaller airtight containers and store in the refrigerator for up to 4 days or freeze for up to 3 months.

IMMUNE-STRENGTHENING CHICKEN BROTH

SERVES: 2

Prep Time: 3 minutes **Cook Time:** 3 minutes

- 3 cups (720 ml) Chicken Bone Broth (page 239)
- 1 tablespoon finely grated ginger
- Pinch of cayenne pepper
- 2 teaspoons lemon juice, or to taste
- Sea salt and freshly ground black pepper
- 1 tablespoon finely chopped flat-leaf parsley leaves

1. Pour the broth into a saucepan and bring to a simmer over medium heat. Add the ginger, cayenne pepper, and lemon juice and stir to combine. Season with salt and pepper.
2. Pour the hot broth into two glasses or mugs and sprinkle over the chopped parsley. Take a sip and enjoy.

FISH BONE BROTH

MAKES: 3 QUARTS (3 LITERS)

Prep Time: 10 minutes **Cook Time:** 3–4 hours

3–4 non-oily fish carcasses and heads (such as snapper, barramundi, or kingfish)
2 celery stalks, roughly chopped
2 onions, roughly chopped
1 carrot, roughly chopped
2 tablespoons apple cider vinegar
1 handful thyme sprigs and flat-leaf parsley stalks
3 fresh bay leaves

1. Place the fish carcasses and heads in a stockpot, add the veggies and vinegar, and cover with 3¾ quarts (3.5 liters) of cold water. Bring to a boil, skimming off the scum that rises to the top.
2. Tie the herbs together with kitchen string and add to the broth. Reduce the heat to low, cover and simmer for 3–4 hours.
3. Remove the fish carcasses and heads with tongs or a slotted spoon. Strain the broth through a fine sieve into storage containers. Cover and cool in the fridge. Remove the congealed fat that rises to the top (it is a fantastic, stable cooking fat) and store it in a glass container in the fridge for up to 2 weeks—use it for frying and sautéing. Transfer the gelatinous broth to smaller airtight containers and store in the fridge for up to 4 days or freeze for up to 3 months.

CHINESE BROTH

MAKES: 3 CUPS (700 ML)

Prep Time: 3 minutes **Cook Time:** 5 minutes

3 cups (700 ml) Chicken Bone Broth (page 239) or Fish Bone Broth (page 241)
1½ tablespoons tamari
1½ teaspoons sesame oil
Sea salt and freshly ground black pepper if needed

Pour the broth into a saucepan and stir in the tamari and sesame oil. Place over medium heat and bring to a simmer to heat through. Taste, and add a little salt and pepper if needed. Store in an airtight container in the fridge for up to 2 weeks or in the freezer for up to 3 months.

PORK BONE BROTH

MAKES 3.7–4 QUARTS (3.5–3.75 LITERS)

Prep Time: 15 minutes (plus 1 hour to soak the bones) **Cook Time:** 12 hours

- About 7.7 pounds (3.5 kg) pork bones and knuckles
- 2 pork trotters (optional)
- 3 tablespoons apple cider vinegar
- 3 onions, roughly chopped
- 3 carrots, roughly chopped
- 3 celery stalks, roughly chopped
- 2 leeks, white part only, roughly chopped
- 3 thyme sprigs
- 2 fresh bay leaves
- 1 teaspoon black peppercorns, crushed
- 1 garlic bulb, halved horizontally
- 2 large handfuls of flat-leaf parsley stalks

1. Place the bones and knuckles and trotters (if using) in a large stockpot, add the vinegar and pour in 5¼ quarts (5 liters) of cold water, or enough to cover. Set aside for 1 hour to help draw out the nutrients from the bones. Remove the bones from the water, reserving the water.
2. Preheat the oven to 350°F (180°C).
3. Transfer all the bones and knuckles and trotters (if using) to a few large roasting tins and roast for 30–40 minutes until browned. Return the bones to the pot and add the veggies.
4. Pour the fat from the roasting tins into a saucepan, add 1 quart (1 liter) of the reserved water, place over high heat and bring to a simmer, stirring with a wooden spoon to loosen any coagulated juices. Add this liquid to the bones and vegetables. If necessary, add the remaining reserved water to the pot to just cover the bones—the liquid should come no higher than ¾ inch (2 cm) below the rim of the pot, as the volume will increase slightly during cooking.
5. Bring the broth to the boil, skimming off the scum that rises to the top. Reduce the heat to low and add the thyme, bay leaves, peppercorns and garlic. Simmer for 12 hours. Just before finishing, add the parsley and simmer for 10 minutes. Strain the broth into a large container, cover and place in the fridge overnight.
6. The next day, remove the congealed fat that has risen to the top and reserve it for cooking; it will keep in the fridge for up to 1 week or in the freezer for up to 3 months.
7. Transfer the gelatinous broth to smaller airtight containers and store in the fridge for up to 4 days or in the freezer for up to 3 months.

MAHA DRESSINGS AND SAUCES: FLAVORFUL FINISHING TOUCHES

Welcome to MAHA's dressings and sauces, where every drizzle and dollop elevates your plate. Think of tangy vinaigrettes, creamy herb blends, or bold, spicy dips that bring dishes to life. This chapter turns simple ingredients into vibrant, budget-friendly condiments that pack a punch. From zesty lemon dressings to rich and delicious mayonnaise options, each recipe adds joy to your meals. Grab a whisk, let your kitchen sing, and craft sauces that make every bite unforgettable.

MAYONNAISE

MAKES: 2 CUPS (500 G)

Prep Time: 10 minutes

4 egg yolks
1½ tablespoons Dijon mustard
1½ tablespoons apple cider vinegar
1 tablespoon lemon juice
1⅔ cups (400 ml) olive oil or macadamia oil, (*or* ¾ cup + 2 tablespoons (200 ml) of each)
Sea salt and freshly ground black pepper

TIP:

Alternatively, you can place the egg yolks, mustard, vinegar, lemon juice, and a pinch of salt in the bowl of a food processor and process until combined. With the motor running, slowly pour in the oil in a thin, steady stream and process until the mayonnaise is thick and creamy. Season with salt and pepper and store as above.

1. Place the egg yolks, mustard, vinegar, lemon juice, oil, and a pinch of salt in a glass jug or jar.
2. Blend with a handheld blender until smooth and creamy, working the blade from the bottom of the jug very slowly up to the top.
3. Season with salt and pepper.
4. Store in a sealed glass jar in the fridge for 4–5 days.

SRIRACHA MAYONNAISE

MAKES: ½ CUP

Prep Time: 2 minutes

1–2 teaspoons sriracha chili sauce (depending on how spicy you like it)
½ cup (120 g) Mayonnaise (to make your own, see page 244)

To make the spicy mayonnaise, place the ingredients in a bowl and mix to combine.

AIOLI

MAKES: ABOUT 2 CUPS (500 G)

Prep Time: 10 minutes

4 organic, free-range egg yolks
1½ tablespoons Dijon mustard
1½ tablespoons apple cider vinegar
1 tablespoon lemon juice
4 cloves roasted garlic
1⅔ cups (400 ml) olive oil or macadamia oil, (or ¾ cup + 2 tablespoons (200 ml) of each)
Sea salt and freshly ground black pepper

1. Place the egg yolks, mustard, vinegar, lemon juice, roasted garlic, oil, and a pinch of salt in a glass jug or jar.
2. Blend with a handheld blender until smooth and creamy, working the blade from the bottom of the jug very slowly up to the top.
3. Season with salt and pepper.
4. Store in a sealed glass jar in the fridge for 4–5 days.

CHIPOTLE AIOLI

MAKES: ABOUT 1 CUP

Prep Time: 2 minutes

1 cup (240 g) aioli (to make your own, see recipe on page 245)
1 chipotle chilies in adobo sauce
1 tablespoon adobo sauce

To make the chipotle aioli, use a handheld blender to blend all the ingredients until smooth. (Add more aioli if the flavor is too spicy for your liking, or add more chipotles if you prefer the aioli to be extra spicy.)

TOMATO KETCHUP

MAKES: ABOUT 1⅓ CUPS (330 ML)

Prep Time: 5 minutes **Cook Time:** 2 minutes

¾ cup (180 g) tomato paste
1 tablespoon apple cider vinegar
1 teaspoon garlic powder
1 teaspoon onion powder
½ teaspoon ground cinnamon
¼ teaspoon freshly grated nutmeg
1 teaspoon honey
Pinch ground cloves

1. Mix the tomato paste with ⅓ cup (90 ml) of water in a small saucepan.
2. Place over medium heat and bring to a simmer (add more water if you prefer your sauce to be thinner). Remove from the heat and stir in the remaining ingredients until incorporated and smooth.
3. Cool and store in an airtight glass jar in the fridge for up to 4 weeks.

HOT SAUCE

MAKES: 2 CUPS (500 ML)

Prep Time: 15–20 minutes **Cook Time:** 30 minutes

- 2 tablespoons coconut oil or good-quality animal fat
- 1 yellow onion, finely chopped
- 6 long red chilies, chopped
- 2–3 habanero chilies, deseeded and chopped
- 4 cloves garlic, finely chopped
- 3 tomatoes, chopped
- ¾ cup (200 ml) apple cider vinegar
- 2 teaspoons sea salt
- 1 tablespoon honey
- 2 tablespoons tamari or coconut aminos

1. Heat the coconut oil or animal fat in a large saucepan over medium heat. Add the onion, chilies, and garlic and cook for 5 minutes, or until softened. Reduce the heat to medium–low, then stir in the tomato, vinegar, salt, honey, tamari or coconut aminos, and 3 tablespoons of water. Simmer, stirring occasionally, for about 30 minutes until the tomato breaks down and the flavor develops. Allow to cool.
2. Transfer the tomato and chili mixture to a blender and blend until smooth. Strain through a fine sieve, if desired, discarding the leftover pulp.
3. Pour the hot sauce into glass jars with screw-top lids and store in the fridge for up to 1 month.

CHIMICHURRI

MAKES: 1¾ CUPS (450 ML)

Prep Time: 10 minutes

- 4 cloves garlic, peeled
- Sea salt
- 1 long red chili, deseeded and finely chopped (leave the seeds in if you like it extra spicy)
- 2 very large handfuls flat-leaf parsley leaves
- 2 very large handfuls cilantro leaves
- ⅓ cup (80 ml) apple cider vinegar
- 1 teaspoon ground cumin
- 1 cup (240 ml) extra-virgin olive oil
- Freshly ground black pepper

1. Place the garlic and a little salt in a mortar and crush with the pestle. Add the chili, parsley, and cilantro and pound to a paste.
2. Stir in the vinegar, cumin, and olive oil, then taste and season with salt and pepper. Alternatively, place the garlic, chili, and herbs in a food processor and process until finely chopped. With the motor running, pour in the vinegar and oil and process to combine. Add the cumin and season with salt and pepper.
3. Store in an airtight container in the fridge for up to 1 week.

BARBECUE SAUCE

MAKES: 1⅔ CUPS (380 G)

Prep Time: 12 minutes **Cook Time:** 10 minutes

⅓ cup + 1 tablespoon (100 g) tomato paste
3 tablespoons apple cider vinegar
1 tablespoon Dijon mustard
⅓ cup + 1 tablespoons (120 g) honey
⅓ cup (100 ml) maple syrup
1 teaspoon smoked paprika
⅓ cup + 1 tablespoon (100 ml) tamari
2 cloves garlic, finely chopped
1 tablespoon liquid smoke, *optional* (see Note)
Pinch ground cloves
1 cinnamon stick
Sea salt, to taste

Place all the ingredients in a saucepan over medium heat, mix well and bring to a simmer. Reduce the heat to low and cook, stirring occasionally, for 10 minutes. Season with salt to taste and leave to cool. Remove the cinnamon stick and store in an airtight bottle in the fridge for up to 2 weeks.

Note:

Liquid smoke is a water-soluble liquid that forms from condensed smoke particles when chips from a hardwood (such as hickory) are burned. You can buy it from some supermarkets, delis, specialty food stores, or online.

COCKTAIL SAUCE

MAKES: ABOUT ½ CUP (120 G)

Prep Time: 2 minutes

⅓ cup plus 1 tablespoon (100 g) Mayonnaise (page 244)
1 tablespoon Tomato Ketchup (page 246)
1 teaspoon Worcestershire sauce
4 drops Tabasco sauce

To make the cocktail sauce, combine all the ingredients in a bowl. Set aside until ready to serve or refrigerate in an airtight container.

NAM JIM

MAKES: ABOUT ¾ CUP (175 ML)

Prep Time: 8–10 minutes

- **4 red Asian shallots, chopped**
- **2 long red chillies, chopped**
- **2 garlic cloves, chopped**
- **1 (1-inch/2.5 cm) piece of ginger, chopped**
- **1 tablespoon washed and finely chopped coriander roots and stalks**
- **10 tablespoons (150 ml) lime juice**
- **1 tablespoon coconut sugar or honey (optional)**
- **2½ tablespoons fish sauce**

To make the nam jim, pound the shallot, chilli, garlic, ginger, and coriander roots and stalks to a paste using a large mortar and pestle. Add the lime juice and mix well. Mix in the sugar or honey (if using) and fish sauce. Taste and adjust the seasoning if necessary, so that the dressing is a balance of hot, sour, salty, and sweet. Strain through a sieve and discard the pulp.

SRIRACHA CHILI SAUCE

MAKES: 2½ CUPS (625 ML)

Prep Time: 15 minutes **Cook Time:** 5–10 minutes

- **1½ pounds (680 g) long red chilies, deseeded and roughly chopped**
- **8 cloves garlic, crushed**
- **½ red bell pepper, deseeded and chopped**
- **⅓ cup (80 ml) apple cider vinegar**
- **2 tablespoons coconut sugar**
- **2 tablespoons fish sauce**
- **Sea salt**

1. Pulse all the ingredients except the salt in a high-speed blender until smooth.
2. Pour into a saucepan and bring to a boil over high heat, stirring occasionally. Reduce the heat to low and simmer, stirring now and then, for 5–10 minutes. Add water to reach your desired consistency and season with salt to taste.
3. Transfer to a large airtight glass jar and store in the fridge for up to 2 weeks.

MINT SAUCE

MAKES: ABOUT 1 CUP (250 ML)

Prep Time: 5 minutes

- 3 large handfuls mint leaves, finely chopped
- 1⁄3 cup (80 ml) apple cider vinegar
- 1 tablespoon honey
- 1⁄3 cup plus 1 tablespoon (100 ml) olive oil
- Sea salt, to taste

1. Place all the ingredients in a bowl and whisk to combine.
2. Store in an airtight glass jar in the fridge for up to 4 days.

RAITA

MAKES: ABOUT 1 CUP (250 G)

Prep Time: 5 minutes

½ Persian cucumber
¾ cup (200 g) coconut yogurt (page 62)
1 teaspoon ground cumin
2 tablespoons finely chopped mint leaves
Sea salt and freshly ground black pepper

1. To make the raita, cut the cucumber in half lengthways and use a teaspoon to scrape out the seeds. Coarsely grate the cucumber flesh and squeeze out the excess liquid with your hands.
2. Combine the cucumber with the yogurt, cumin, and mint in a bowl and stir well. Season to taste.

ITALIAN DRESSING

MAKES: ABOUT 1¼ CUPS (300 ML)

Prep Time: 3 minutes

⅓ cup (80 ml) balsamic vinegar
¾ cup (200 ml) extra-virgin olive oil
10 basil leaves, finely chopped (you can also use micro basil leaves)
1 teaspoon finely chopped oregano leaves
Sea salt and freshly ground black pepper

1. Combine the balsamic vinegar, olive oil, basil, and oregano in a large bowl whisk well. Season with salt and pepper.
2. Store in an airtight glass jar in the fridge for up to 5 days.

SOUTH AMERICAN DRESSING

MAKES: ABOUT 1 CUP (250 ML)

Prep Time: 5 minutes

⅓ cup (30 g) (about 1 bunch) chopped cilantro leaves
½ cup (120 ml) lime juice
½ cup (120 ml) extra-virgin olive oil
Sea salt and freshly ground black pepper

1. Place the cilantro, lime juice, and olive oil in a bowl and mix to combine. Season with salt and pepper.
2. Store in an airtight glass jar in the fridge for up to 1 week.

BACON AND SHERRY VINAIGRETTE

MAKES: 1¼ CUPS (280 ML)

Prep Time: 5 minutes **Cook Time:** 5 minutes

- **½ French shallot, finely chopped**
- **Coconut oil, for cooking**
- **4¼ ounces (120 g) free-range bacon, finely diced**
- **3 tablespoons sherry vinegar or apple cider vinegar**
- **1 tablespoon Dijon mustard**
- **1 teaspoon finely chopped chives**
- **⅓ cup plus 1 tablespoon (100 ml) extra-virgin olive oil**
- **Sea salt and freshly ground black pepper**

1. In a small saucepan over low heat, gently cook the shallots with a little oil until soft, for about 5 minutes. Remove from the pan, wipe the pan dry with a kitchen towel, and place back over a medium heat.
2. Add a little more oil and then add the bacon. Fry the bacon, stirring occasionally for 6–8 minutes or until crispy and golden.
3. Add the vinegar and shallots and set aside to cool.
4. Transfer to a bowl and whisk in the mustard, chives and olive oil, and season with sea salt and pepper.

KRAUT AND HERB DRESSING

MAKES: ½ CUP (120 ML)

Prep Time: 5 minutes

- ⅓ cup (80 ml) extra-virgin olive oil
- 2 tablespoons sauerkraut brine (from your homemade kraut—see page 268), extra if needed
- 2 tablespoons Sauerkraut, finely chopped (page 268)
- 1 tablespoon apple cider vinegar
- 1 teaspoon Dijon mustard
- ½ teaspoon honey
- 1 tablespoon finely chopped fresh herbs (e.g. tarragon, parsley, dill, or a mixture)
- Sea salt and freshly cracked black pepper, to taste

1. In a small bowl or jar, whisk together the olive oil, sauerkraut brine, chopped sauerkraut, vinegar, mustard, and honey.
2. Stir in the fresh herbs and season with salt and pepper.
3. Taste and adjust the balance—add more brine or apple cider vinegar for tang if desired, or a splash of oil to mellow it.
4. Use immediately or refrigerate for up to 3 days. Shake or whisk well before using.

FERMENTED MUSTARD HERB DRESSING

MAKES: ½ CUP (125 ML)

Prep Time: 5 minutes

⅓ cup (80 ml) extra-virgin olive oil
2 tablespoons sauerkraut brine (from homemade kraut or store-bought)
2 tablespoon whole-grain mustard
1 tablespoon apple cider vinegar
½ small clove garlic, finely grated
½ teaspoon honey
2 tablespoons finely chopped fresh herbs (such as dill, parsley, chives, or tarragon, or a mixture)
Sea salt and freshly ground black pepper, to taste

1. In a small bowl or jar, whisk together the olive oil, sauerkraut brine, fermented mustard, vinegar, garlic, and honey until well combined.
2. Stir in the fresh herbs. Taste and season with sea salt and black pepper. Add more brine or apple cider vinegar for extra tang, or a splash more oil to mellow it.
3. Serve immediately, or refrigerate in a sealed jar for up to 3 days. Shake or stir before each use.

AVOCADO PUREE

MAKES: ⅔ CUP (160 G)

Prep Time: 5 minutes

- **1 avocado, stone removed**
- **1 tablespoon lemon juice**
- **Sea salt and freshly ground black pepper**

To make the avocado puree, place the avocado and lemon juice in the bowl of a food processor and blend until smooth and creamy. Season with salt and pepper. Transfer to a bowl and set aside until needed.

GUACAMOLE

SERVES: 4

Prep Time: 10 minutes

2½ avocados, diced
1 long red chili, halved lengthways, deseeded and finely chopped, plus extra to serve, *optional*
Juice of 1 lime, plus extra to taste (or use the equivalent amount of sauerkraut juice)
1 tablespoon finely diced red onion
1 tablespoon chopped cilantro leaves
1 tablespoon extra-virgin olive oil
Sea salt and freshly ground black pepper

Combine the avocado, chili, lime juice, onion, cilantro, and olive oil in a small bowl and gently mix. Season with salt and pepper and sprinkle over the extra chili (if using). Taste and add a little more lime juice, if you like.

CASHEW SOUR CREAM

MAKES: 2 CUPS (500 ML)

Prep Time: 5–10 minutes (2–4 hours soaking time)

1 cup (155 g) cashews
Juice from 1 lemon, extra if desired
¾ cup (200 ml) filtered water

Note:

This needs to be prepared overnight.

1. Pinch salt
2. Soak the cashews in 3 cups (750 ml) of water for at least 2–4 hours. Drain and rinse well.
3. Place the cashews in a food processor or a high-speed blender; add the lemon juice water and salt and blend until smooth and creamy. Pour in more water slowly until you reach your desired consistency. Add a little more lemon juice if you like the sour cream to be tangier.

PORK JUS

MAKES: 2¾ CUPS (650 ML)

Prep Time: 10 minutes **Cook Time:** 3½ hours

- 2 French shallots, chopped
- 6 thyme sprigs
- 1¼ cups (300 ml) dry white wine (such as sauvignon blanc)
- 1 tablespoon Dijon mustard
- 3 quarts (3 liters) Pork Bone Broth (page 242)
- 1½ teaspoons tapioca flour mixed with 1 tablespoon water, *optional*
- Sea salt and freshly ground black pepper

1. Place the shallot and thyme in a large, heavy-based saucepan and pour in the wine. Bring to a boil over medium–high heat and simmer until reduced by two-thirds.
2. Mix in the mustard, then pour in the broth and return to a boil. Reduce the heat to medium and simmer, occasionally skimming the scum that rises to the surface, until the jus has reduced by three-quarters to a sauce-like consistency. If the jus is still a little too thin, you can thicken it slightly by whisking in the tapioca mixture and simmering until it coats the back of a spoon.
3. Strain through a sieve and season with salt and pepper.
4. Store in an airtight container in the fridge for up to 5 days or freeze for up to 3 months.

PIZZA SAUCE

MAKES: 1⅔ CUP (400 ML)

Prep Time: 5 minutes

- 14½-ounce (400-g) can or jar whole peeled tomatoes (see Note page 105)
- 1 teaspoon dried oregano
- 2 pinches of freshly ground black pepper sea salt

1. Combine all the ingredients in a food processor and process until smooth. Season with salt to taste.
2. Store in an airtight container in the fridge for up to 4 days.

MAHA SPICE BLENDS: IGNITE YOUR DISHES

Step into MAHA's world of spice blends, where vibrant flavors transform every meal. Picture aromatic mixes of smoky paprika, warm cumin, or zesty citrus notes, crafted to elevate simple ingredients. This chapter offers budget-friendly blends that add soul to any dish, from grilled meats to roasted veggies. Mix up a bold rub or a fragrant sprinkle, let your kitchen hum with creativity, and make every bite a flavorful adventure.

BARBECUE SPICE BLEND

MAKES: 1 CUP (140 G)

Prep Time: 2 minutes

½ cup (60 g) sea salt flakes
3 tablespoons smoked paprika
2 tablespoons onion powder
1 tablespoon garlic powder

1. Place all the ingredients in a bowl and mix to combine.
2. Store in an airtight container in the pantry for up to 3 months

FURIKAKE SEASONING

MAKES: ¼ CUP (30 G)

Prep Time: 3 minutes

2 nori sheets, torn or snipped into 1-inch (2.5-cm) pieces
2 teaspoons sea salt
3 tablespoons bonito flakes
Pinch coconut sugar, *optional*
1½ tablespoons sesame seeds, toasted

Place the nori, salt, and bonito flakes in a blender and pulse a few times to finely chop the nori. Mix in the sugar (if using) and toasted sesame seeds and set aside until needed. Store in an airtight container in the pantry for up to 3 months.

HEALING SPICE BLEND

MAKES: ABOUT ⅔ CUP (90 G)

Prep Time: 2 minutes

½ cup (65 g) sea salt flakes
1 tablespoon ground turmeric
2 teaspoons ground ginger
2 teaspoons garlic powder

Place all the ingredients in a bowl and mix to combine. Store in an airtight container in the pantry for up to 3 months.

INDIAN SPICE BLEND

MAKES: ¾ CUP (120 G)

Prep Time: 2 minutes

⅔ cup (80 g) sea salt flakes
3 tablespoons curry powder
1 teaspoon ground ginger
1 teaspoon garlic powder

Place all the ingredients in a bowl and mix to combine. Store in an airtight container in the pantry for up to 3 months.

STEAK SEASONING

MAKES: ABOUT 1 CUP (90 G)

Prep Time: 2 minutes

3 teaspoons chilli flakes
1½ tablespoons finely chopped rosemary leaves (or dried rosemary: 1¼ teaspoons)
2 teaspoons finely grated lemon zest
¾ cup (80 g) sea salt flakes

Place all the ingredients in a bowl and mix to combine. Store in an airtight container in the pantry for up to 3 months.

PORK SEASONING

MAKES: 1 CUP (120 G)

Prep Time: 5 minutes **Cook Time:** 1 hour

⅔ cup (80 g) sea salt flakes
2 tablespoons finely chopped sage leaves
2½ tablespoons crushed fennel seeds
1½ tablespoons ground cumin

1. Preheat the oven to 140°F / 60°C or the lowest possible setting. Line a baking tray with baking paper.
2. Place all the ingredients in a bowl and mix to combine. Spread the mixture on the prepared tray in an even layer and bake for 1 hour, or until completely dry. Allow to cool. Store in an airtight container in the pantry for up to 3 months.

FERMENTED VEGETABLES AND PICKLES AT MAHA: TANGY TREASURES

Unlock the tangy magic of MAHA's fermented vegetables and pickles, where simple produce becomes a flavor explosion. Envision crunchy cabbage kimchi with a spicy kick, pickled Indonesian vegetables that pop, or colorful turmeric kraut bubbling with life. This chapter guides you through easy, budget-friendly ferments that boost health and add zest to any meal. Grab your mason jars or fermentation crocks, slice up some fresh veggies, and let's dive into the art of fermentation, creating probiotic wonders that make your kitchen fizz with excitement.

KID-FRIENDLY KIMCHI

MAKES: 1½ QUARTS (1.5 L)

Prep Time: 20 minutes (plus 10–14 days to ferment)

- **1 pound (450 g) red cabbage**
- **1 pound (450 g) green cabbage**
- **3½ ounces (100 g) daikon (white radish), diced**
- **1 green apple, cored and julienned**
- **1 red onion, thinly sliced**
- **1 French shallot, thinly sliced**
- **1 handful cilantro leaves, chopped**
- **Juice of 1 lemon**
- **1½ teaspoons sea salt**
- **1 sachet vegetable starter culture (¼–½ teaspoon (2–5 g), depending on the brand)**

Note:

You will need a 1½ quart (1.5 liter) preserving jar with an airlock lid for this recipe.

1. Wash the jar and all the utensils you will be using in very hot water. Dry well and set aside. Alternatively, run them through a hot rinse cycle in the dishwasher.
2. Remove the outer leaves of the cabbages. Choose an unblemished leaf, wash it well, and set aside for later. Shred the cabbages in a food processor or slice with a knife or mandoline, then transfer to a large glass or stainless steel bowl. Add the daikon, apple, onion, shallot, cilantro, lemon juice, and salt and mix well. Cover and set aside.
3. Prepare the starter culture according to the directions on the packet. Add to the vegetables and mix thoroughly. Using a large spoon, fill the prepared jar with the vegetable mixture, pressing down to remove any air pockets and leaving ¾ inch (2 cm) of room at the top. The vegetables should be completely submerged in the liquid. Add more water if necessary.
4. Take the clean cabbage leaf, fold it up, and place it on top of the mixture, then add a small glass weight (a shot glass is ideal) to keep everything submerged. Close the lid, then wrap a tea towel around the side of the jar to block out the light.
5. Store the jar in a dark place with a temperature of 60–74°F (16–23°C) for 10–14 days. You can place the jar in a cooler to maintain a more consistent temperature. Different vegetables have different culturing times, and the warmer it is the shorter the time needed. The longer you leave it to ferment, the higher the level of good bacteria and the tangier the flavor.
6. Chill before eating. Once opened, the kimchi will last for up to 2 months in the fridge when kept submerged in liquid. If unopened, it will keep for up to 9 months in the fridge.

TURMERIC KRAUT

MAKES: 1 QUART (1 LITER)

Prep Time: 15 minutes (plus 12–14 days to ferment)

1½ pounds (600 g) cabbage (you can use green or red, or a mixture of the two)
2 cups (200 g) grated carrot
2 tablespoons finely chopped ginger
2 (2-inch / 5-cm) pieces fresh turmeric, finely chopped, or 1 tablespoon ground turmeric
2 teaspoons caraway seeds
2 tablespoons fine sea salt
Filtered water, *optional*

Note:

You will need a 1 quart (1 liter) preserving jar with an airlock lid for this recipe. Wash the jar and all the utensils you will be using in very hot water or run them through a hot rinse cycle in the dishwasher.

1. Remove the outer leaves of the cabbage. Choose an unblemished outer leaf, wash it well and set aside.
2. Shred the cabbage in a food processor or slice with a knife or mandoline.
3. Place the shredded cabbage, carrot, ginger, turmeric, and caraway seeds in a glass or stainless-steel bowl, then sprinkle on the salt. Mix well and massage with very clean hands (or you can wear gloves) for 10 minutes to release some liquid.
4. Using a large spoon, fill the prepared jar with the cabbage mixture, pressing down well to remove any air pockets and leaving ¾ inch (2 cm) of room free at the top. The vegetables should be completely submerged in the liquid; top up with filtered water, if necessary.
5. Fold up the clean reserved cabbage leaf and place it on top of the cabbage mixture, then add a small glass weight (a shot glass is ideal) to keep everything submerged. Close the lid and wrap a tea towel around the jar to block out the light; leave the airlock exposed. Store in a dark place (such as a cooler) at 60–74°F (16–23°C) for 12–14 days.
6. Chill before eating. Once opened, the turmeric kraut, submerged in the liquid, will keep in the fridge for up to 2 months. Unopened, it will keep for up to 9 months in the fridge. Reserve the brine; it can be used to make a delicious salad dressing.

SAUERKRAUT

MAKES: 1½ QUARTS (1.5 L)

Prep Time: 15 minutes (plus 10–14 days fermenting)

1 star anise
1 teaspoon whole cloves
1½ pounds (650 g) cabbage (green or red, or a mix of the two)
1½ teaspoons sea salt
2 teaspoons caraway seeds
2 tablespoons juniper berries
1 small handful dill, roughly chopped
1 sachet vegetable starter culture (⅛ ounce / 5 g, depending on the brand)

Note:

You will need a 1.5 quart (1.5L) preserving jar with an airlock lid for this recipe. Wash the jar and utensils thoroughly in very hot water or run them through a hot rinse cycle in the dishwasher.

1. Place the star anise and cloves in a small piece of muslin, tie into a bundle, and set aside.
2. Remove the outer leaves of the cabbage. Choose one of the outer leaves, wash it well, and set aside. Shred the cabbage in a food processor or slice by hand or with a mandoline, then place in a large glass or stainless steel bowl.
3. Sprinkle the salt, caraway seeds, juniper berries, and dill over the cabbage. Mix well, cover, and set aside while you prepare the starter culture.
4. Dissolve the starter culture in water according to the packet instructions (the amount of water will depend on the brand you are using). Add to the cabbage with the muslin bag containing the spices and mix well.
5. Fill the prepared jar with the cabbage mix, pressing down firmly between each addition with a large spoon or potato masher to remove any air pockets. Leave ¾ inch (2 cm) of room free at the top. The cabbage should be completely submerged in the liquid, so add more water if necessary.
6. Take the clean cabbage leaf, fold it up, and place it on top of the mixture, then add a small glass weight to keep everything submerged (a small shot glass is ideal). Close the lid, then wrap a tea towel around the side of the jar to block out the light. Store in a dark place with a temperature of 61–75°F (16–23°C) for at least 10 days and up to 2 weeks. (You can place the jar in a cooler to maintain a more consistent temperature.) Different vegetables have different culturing times and the warmer it is the shorter the time needed.

The longer you leave the jar to ferment, the greater the level of good bacteria will be present. It's up to you how long you leave it—some people prefer the tangier flavor that comes with extra fermenting time, while others prefer a milder flavor.

7. Chill before eating. Once opened, it will last for up to 2 months in the fridge when kept submerged in the liquid. If unopened, it will keep for up to 9 months in the fridge.

PICKLED RED ONION

MAKES: ABOUT 1¼ CUPS (300 G)

Prep Time: 5 minutes **Cook Time:** 2 minutes

1 red onion, cut into 12 wedges
½ cup (120 ml) red wine vinegar
2 fresh or dry bay leaves
1 tablespoon honey
Sea salt and freshly ground black pepper

1. Place the onion, vinegar, bay leaves, and honey in a small saucepan and bring to a simmer over medium heat.
2. Cover with the lid and cook for 1 minute, then remove from the heat and allow to cool completely.
3. Season with salt and pepper.
4. Store in a sterilized airtight glass jar in the refrigerator for up to 2 months.

PALEO ACHAR (INDONESIAN PICKLED VEGETABLES)

SERVES: 4–6

Prep Time: 15 minutes **Pickle Time:** 4 hours or overnight

- **1 carrot, cut into 2-inch (5-cm) batons**
- **1 small zucchini, cut into 2-inch (5-cm) batons**
- **7-ounce (200-g) pineapple, cut into small bite-size pieces**
- **7-ounce (200-g) green cabbage, roughly chopped**
- **1 small cucumber, deseeded and cut into 2-inch (5-cm) batons**
- **1 red chili, deseeded and finely chopped**
- **1¼ cups (300 ml) apple cider vinegar**
- **¾ cup (180 ml) water**
- **3 tablespoons honey**
- **1 tablespoon tamari or coconut aminos**
- **3 garlic cloves, finely chopped**
- **1 tablespoon finely grated ginger**
- **1 teaspoon ground turmeric**
- **1 teaspoon sea salt**
- **To serve (*optional*): Toasted sesame seeds and extra sliced red chili**

1. Add the carrot, zucchini, pineapple, cabbage, cucumber, and chili to a large mixing bowl.
2. In a medium saucepan, combine the vinegar, water, honey, tamari or coconut aminos, garlic, ginger, turmeric, and salt. Bring to a simmer over medium heat. Stir in the vegetable and pineapple mixture, cover with lid and simmer for 2 minutes until slightly tender.
3. Remove from heat and allow to cool, then transfer to a clean jar or airtight container.
4. Refrigerate for at least 4 hours, or overnight for best flavor.
5. Serve chilled, topped with sesame seeds and extra chili if desired.

MISCELLANEOUS MAHA RECIPES: SURPRISES FROM THE PANTRY

Explore MAHA's catch-all chapter, packed with fun, unexpected gems from your kitchen staples. Think satisfying gluten-free bread recipes, homemade ghee for some nourishment, slow-cooked garlic confit to give your meals a special little something. Budget-friendly and endlessly adaptable, these recipes spark creativity for any occasion. Grab what's on hand, stir up some magic, and discover new favorites.

ACTIVATED NUTS AND SEEDS

Activating nuts and seeds helps initiate the sprouting process, reducing enzyme inhibitors and making them much easier to digest.

To activate:

1. Place your nuts or seeds in a bowl and cover with filtered water.
2. Soak according to the type of nut or seed—the harder the nut, the longer the soak:
   - Cashews: 2–4 hours
   - Pecans, Walnuts, Pistachios: 4–6 hours
   - Pine Nuts, Pumpkin Seeds, Sunflower Seeds: 7–10 hours
   - Brazil Nuts, Macadamias: 8 hours
   - Almonds: At least 12 hours
3. After soaking, the nuts or seeds will look plump and may begin to sprout. Rinse thoroughly under running water and pat dry with a clean towel.
4. If desired, season the nuts or seeds with a couple of teaspoons of sea salt or any spice blend you like. Stir well to coat.
5. To dry: Use a dehydrator or your oven set to the lowest temperature (about 120°F / 50°C). Dry for 6 to 24 hours, depending on the nut or seed and your desired texture.
6. Storage: Once completely dry, store in an airtight container in the pantry for up to 3 months.

SALT AND VINEGAR ROASTED NUTS AND SEEDS

MAKES: 3½ CUPS

Prep Time: 10 minutes **Cook Time:** 25 minutes

- ½ cup Brazil nuts, activated if possible
- ½ cup hazelnuts, activated if possible
- ½ cup macadamias, activated if possible
- 1 cup almonds, activated if possible
- ½ cup pepitas (pumpkin seeds)
- ½ cup sunflower seeds
- 3 tablespoons apple cider vinegar
- 2 tablespoons coconut oil, melted
- 1½ teaspoons flaky sea salt

1. Preheat the oven to 300°F (150°C). Line a baking sheet with parchment paper.
2. In a large bowl, toss together the Brazil nuts, hazelnuts, macadamias, almonds, pepitas, and sunflower seeds. Drizzle with apple cider vinegar and melted coconut oil. Sprinkle with sea salt and toss to coat thoroughly.
3. Spread the mixture in a single layer on the prepared baking sheet. Roast for 20–25 minutes, stirring once halfway through, until golden and fragrant.
4. Allow to cool completely on the tray. Once fully cooled, transfer to an airtight jar and store at room temperature for up to 2 weeks.

HOMEMADE GHEE

MAKES: ABOUT 1½ CUPS (350 G)

Prep Time: 5 minutes **Cook Time:** 25–30 minutes

1 pound (450 g) unsalted butter, preferably grass-fed

1. Add the butter to a medium saucepan and melt over low heat.
2. Let it simmer gently. It will start to bubble and separate—foam on top, milk solids on the bottom.
3. Skim off the foam as it forms.
4. Keep cooking until the milk solids at the bottom turn golden and the butter smells rich and nutty (about 25–30 minutes total).
5. Remove from heat and carefully strain the clear golden liquid through a fine sieve or cheesecloth into a clean jar.
6. Let it cool completely, then seal. Store in the fridge for up to 1 month.

RENDERED ANIMAL FAT

MAKES: UP TO 1⅓ POUNDS (600 G)

Prep Time: 10 minutes **Cooking Time:** 3½–4 hours

2¼ pounds (1 kg) pork back fat, beef fat, lamb fat, duck skin or chicken skin (see Note)
½ cup (125 ml) filtered water

NOTE

You can buy pork, beef and lamb fat or duck and chicken skin from your local butcher. They may need to be ordered in advance.

1. If using pork, beef or lamb fat, trim any flesh from the fat with a sharp knife and cut the fat into 1-inch (2½-cm) cubes.
2. Place the fat or skin and water in a large heavy-based saucepan over low heat and simmer, stirring occasionally (taking care as the fat may spit), for 3½–4 hours until the water has evaporated and the fat is golden brown and liquefied. Try and keep the fat at around 212°F (100°C). Use a candy thermometer to test the temperature. You will notice little solid bits of brown crackling floating to the surface and a lot of clear liquid; this is an indication that the fat has rendered and is ready to be taken off the heat.
3. Allow the rendered fat to cool a little before straining through a fine-mesh sieve into a jug, jars, containers, or ice-cube trays. Save the leftover crackling bits as they make a delicious snack. The cooled melted fat will be creamy white in color. Store covered in the fridge for up to 3 months or freeze for up to 9 months.

CRISPY CURRY LEAVES

MAKES: 4 SPRIGS

Prep Time: 2 minutes **Cook Time:** 1 minute

2/3 cup (150 ml) melted coconut oil
4 fresh curry leaf sprigs
Sea salt

1. Melt the coconut oil in a skillet over medium heat.
2. Cooking in batches of two sprigs at a time, fry the curry leaves for 4–5 seconds until crisp. Remove with a slotted spoon and drain on paper towel. Season with salt.

CRISPY SHALLOTS

MAKES: ABOUT 3 TABLESPOONS

Prep Time: 3 minutes **Cook Time:** 2–3 minutes

1 cup (240 ml) melted coconut oil or good-quality animal fat
6–8 French shallots, finely sliced

Melt the coconut oil or fat in a small saucepan over medium heat. Add the shallots and cook for 2–3 minutes until golden. Remove with a slotted spoon and drain on paper towel. (You can re-use the oil for sautéing vegetables or cooking meat, chicken, or fish.) Store the crispy shallots in an airtight container in the pantry for up to 1 month.

GARLIC CONFIT

MAKES: 25 CLOVES

Prep Time: 5 minutes **Cook Time:** 1 hour

25 garlic cloves, peeled
1 cup (240 ml) melted coconut oil

Place the garlic and oil in a saucepan over very low heat (do not allow the oil to boil). Gently poach for 1 hour, or until the garlic is beautifully soft. Transfer the garlic and oil to a sterilized glass jar (see page 266 fermented krauts for instructions), seal, and store in the fridge for up to 3 months.

NUT-FREE PALEO ROLLS

Round Rolls

MAKES: 6

Prep Time: 30 minutes **Cook Time:** 1 hour

1 cup (85 g) psyllium husks
½ cup (70 g) coconut flour, plus extra for dusting
3 tablespoons chia seeds
3 tablespoons flaxseeds
¼ cup (30 g) pumpkin seeds, plus 80 g extra, for sprinkling, *optional*
3 tablespoons sesame seeds
¼ cup (30 g) sunflower seeds
1 tablespoon coconut sugar or honey
2½ teaspoons baking powder
1½ teaspoons sea salt
1 tablespoon apple cider vinegar
3 eggs
2 tablespoons coconut oil, melted

1. Preheat the oven to 350°F (180°C) (320°C / 160°C fan-forced/convection).
2. Line a baking tray with parchment paper.
3. Place the psyllium husks, coconut flour, chia seeds, flaxseeds, pumpkin seeds, sesame seeds, and sunflower seeds in the bowl of a food processor and whiz for a few seconds until the seeds are finely chopped.
4. Transfer the flour mixture to a large bowl, then mix in the coconut sugar or honey, the baking powder, and salt.
5. In another bowl, combine the vinegar, 1 pint (450 ml) of water, and the eggs and whisk until smooth. Add the coconut oil and the egg mixture to the dry ingredients and mix well to form a wet dough. Allow to stand for 2 minutes.
6. Knead the dough on a lightly floured work surface for 1 minute.
7. Divide the dough into six portions and roll into balls.
8. Place the dough balls on the prepared tray, allowing room for spreading. Sprinkle with the extra pumpkin seeds if you like. Bake in the oven for 1 hour, rotating the tray halfway through so the rolls cook evenly. To check if they are cooked, tap the base of a roll. If it sounds hollow, the rolls are ready. If they seem to be very heavy and dense, they need to cook for a little longer.

Long Rolls

MAKES: 6

1. Follow the steps above for preparing and kneading the dough. Divide the dough into six portions and roll into 5-inch (12-cm) long log shapes. Place on the prepared tray, allowing room for spreading, and bake in the oven for 1 hour, rotating the tray halfway through so the rolls cook evenly. To check if they are cooked, tap the base of a roll. If it sounds hollow, the rolls are ready. If they seem to be very heavy and dense, they need to cook for a little longer.
2. Dust with a little coconut flour, if desired.

Baguettes

MAKES: 2

1. Follow the steps on the previous page for preparing and kneading the dough. Divide the dough into two portions and roll into 12–14-inch (30–35-cm) log shapes. Place the dough portions on the prepared tray, allowing room for spreading.
2. Cut four or five ½-inch (1 cm) deep diagonal slits across the top of each baguette. This is mainly decorative, so if you like you can skip this step. Bake in the oven for 1 hour, rotating the tray halfway through so the baguettes cook evenly.
3. To check if they are cooked, tap the base of a baguette. If it sounds hollow, they are ready. If they seem to be very heavy and dense, cook for a little longer.

PALEO HEMP BREAD LOAF

MAKES 1 8 × 4 INCH (20 CM) LOAF (10–12 SLICES)

Prep Time: 25 minutes **Cook Time:** 1½ hours

1 cup (145 g) hemp seeds (see Note)
1 cup (170 g) golden or brown flaxseeds
1 cup (240 ml) hot water
½ cup (40 g) psyllium husks
3 tablespoons coconut flour, plus extra for dusting
8 eggs
1 tablespoon apple cider vinegar
1 teaspoon sesame oil
1 teaspoon bicarbonate of soda
1½ teaspoons fine sea salt

1. Place the hemp seeds and flaxseeds in a bowl, pour in the hot water and stir well. Allow to soak for 1 hour at room temperature (the seeds will expand and absorb the water).
2. Preheat the oven to 340°F (170°C) or 300°F (150°C fan-forced/convection). Grease a 8 × 4-inch (20 cm × 10 cm) loaf pan and line the base and sides with baking paper, cutting into the corners to fit.
3. Transfer the soaked seed mixture to the bowl of a food processor and process for 2 minutes, scraping down the side regularly to ensure the mix blends evenly, until a wet dough forms. Next, add the psyllium husks and coconut flour and blend until well combined. Add the eggs, vinegar, sesame oil, bicarbonate of soda and salt and blend for about 1 minute to form a thick dough.
4. Place the dough in the prepared tin and pat down. Bake for 1½ hours, rotating the tin halfway through so the loaf cooks evenly. To check if the bread is cooked, insert a skewer in the center; if it comes out clean, it's ready. Allow the bread to cool a little in the tin before turning out onto a wire rack to cool completely. Cut into thick slices to serve.
5. Store in an airtight container in the fridge for up to 5 days or sliced in the freezer for up to 3 months.

Note:

You can purchase hemp seeds from health-food stores and online.

FLATBREADS

MAKES: 7

Prep Time: 5 minutes **Cook Time:** 15 minutes

1⅔ cups (170 g) almond meal
1 cup (125 g) tapioca flour
½ teaspoon baking powder
½ cup (125 ml) coconut milk
3 organic, free-range eggs
½ teaspoon sea salt
Coconut oil or good-quality animal fat, for cooking

1. Combine the almond meal, tapioca flour, baking powder, coconut milk, eggs, salt, and ½ cup (125 ml) of water in a bowl.
2. Heat a small nonstick skillet over medium heat. Add enough coconut oil or fat to coat the base of the skillet, then pour in ⅓ cup (80 ml) of batter and swirl around. Cook for 2 minutes, or until mostly cooked through, then flip and cook for 1 minute, or until golden and crisp. Place the flatbread on a plate and repeat with the remaining mixture.
3. Store the flatbreads in an airtight container in the fridge for up to 1 week or freeze for up to 3 months.

WHIPPED COCONUT CREAM

MAKES: 3 CUPS (740 ML)

Prep Time: 5 minutes (plus chill coconut ceam overnight)

3⅓ cups (800 ml) coconut cream
2 tablespoons honey, or to taste

1. Place the unopened containers of coconut cream in a stainless-steel bowl and refrigerate overnight.
2. Open the containers of chilled coconut cream and scoop the contents into another bowl. Separate the hardened cream layer from the water layer. Place the cream layer and the honey in the chilled bowl. (Store the coconut water in a sealed container in the fridge for another use.)
3. Use an electric mixer to whip the coconut cream and honey on high speed for about 3 minutes, or until soft peaks form. Allow to set for 40 minutes in the fridge before using.

RASPBERRY AND CHIA SAUCE

MAKES: 1 CUP

Prep Time: 5 minutes

2 teaspoons chia seeds
1¾ cups (250 g) frozen raspberries, thawed
2 tablespoons finely ground monk fruit sweetener or xylitol

1. Place all the raspberry and chia sauce ingredients in a bowl.
2. Stir, making sure the chia seeds are moistened with the juice from the raspberries. Place in a food processor and pulse two or three times to break up the berries. Transfer to the fridge to chill until ready to use.

KALE CHIPS

SERVES: 2–4

Prep Time: 5 minutes **Cook Time:** 40 minutes

1 bunch of kale (about 12 ounces / 350 g)
1 tablespoon coconut oil, melted
½ teaspoon of your favorite spice (such as curry powder, ras el hanout, smoked paprika, ground cumin, or ground turmeric), *optional*
Sea salt

1. Preheat the oven to 250°F (120°C) or 230°F (100°C fan-forced/convection). Line a baking sheet with parchment paper.
2. Wash the kale thoroughly in cold water and pat dry. Remove and discard the tough central stems, then cut the leaves into smaller pieces.
3. In a large bowl, toss the kale with some coconut oil, spice (if using), and salt—go easy on the salt as a little goes a long way. Spread the kale on the baking tray in a single layer; do not overcrowd. Use more than one baking tray, if required. Roast the kale for 35–40 minutes until crispy. Serve immediately or store in an airtight container in the pantry for up to 2 weeks.

SEMI-DRIED TOMATOES

MAKES: 1½ CUPS (350 G)

Prep Time: 10 mins **Cook Time:** 1½ hours

1 pound (450 g) tomatoes, quartered
Sea salt and freshly ground black pepper
1½ teaspoons dried oregano
⅓ cup + 1 tablespoon (100 ml) extra-virgin olive oil

1. Preheat the oven to 250°F (120°C). Line a baking sheet with parchment paper and place a wire rack on the tray.
2. Arrange the tomatoes, cut-side up, on the wire rack. Season the tomatoes with salt and pepper and sprinkle on the dried oregano. Bake in the oven for 1½ hours, or until the tomatoes are dry around the edges but still soft in the centre. Set aside to cool completely. Transfer the tomatoes to a sterilised glass jar, pour in the olive oil, seal, and store in the fridge for up to 2 weeks.

SWEET POTATO MASH

SERVES: 4 AS A SIDE

Prep Time: 10 minutes **Cook Time:** 30 minutes

1½ pounds (680 g) sweet potato, peeled and cut into chunks
1 clove garlic, peeled
⅓ cup (80 ml) coconut milk
1 tablespoon melted ghee or extra-virgin olive oil
Pinch sea salt
Freshly ground black pepper
Chopped cilantro leaves, to serve, *optional*

1. Place the sweet potatoes and garlic in a saucepan. Cover with cold water and bring to a boil. Reduce the heat to low, cover with a lid, and simmer for 30 minutes, or until tender. Drain well and transfer to a food processor.
2. Add the coconut milk and melted ghee or olive oil. Blend until smooth. Season with salt and pepper to taste.
3. Spoon into a serving bowl, sprinkle with chopped cilantro if using, and serve immediately.

CAULIFLOWER RICE

SERVES: 4–6

Prep Time: 5 minutes **Cook Time:** 6 minutes

1 head of cauliflower (about 2¼ pounds / 1 kg), florets and stems roughly chopped
2 tablespoons coconut oil or good-quality animal fat
Sea salt and freshly ground black pepper

1. Place the cauliflower in the bowl of a food processor and pulse into tiny, fine pieces that look like rice.
2. Melt the coconut oil or fat in a large skillet over medium heat.
3. Add the cauliflower and cook for 4–6 minutes until softened.
4. Season with salt and pepper and serve.

PISTACHIO GREMOLATA

MAKES: ABOUT ½ CUP (130 G)

Prep Time: 5 minutes (plus 15 minutes for the flavors to develop)

- **½ cup (20 g) finely chopped flat-leaf parsley leaves**
- **3 tablespoons finely chopped toasted pistachio kernels**
- **1 clove garlic, finely chopped**
- **Zest and juice of ½ lemon, or to taste**
- **Sea salt and freshly ground black pepper**
- **3 tablespoons extra-virgin olive oil**

1. Combine all the ingredients in a small bowl and set aside for 15 minutes to allow the flavors to develop.
2. Store in an airtight container in the fridge for up to 5 days.

Acknowledgments

It is with my deepest bow of love and gratitude that I honor the many wonderful beings in my life that inspire and support my path. Beginning with my beautiful wife Nic, my loving partner in this earthly experience, thank you, my love, for showing up in your wild authenticity; your presence is pure grace. I love you. Also, I'm forever thankful for the two young women who gifted me the absolutely amazing journey of fatherhood, Chilli and Indii, thank you for being your unique selves and for living life the way you both choose to live; it is an honor to witness you both shine.

To Monica and Jacinta Cannataci, you have both been instrumental in my journey as a chef. Everything you create, both together and as individuals, is joy to behold. The zest you have both woven into this book is forever held in reverence.

To the talented photographers and food stylists that I have had the pleasure of working with over the years. I'm always beyond stoked with the beauty you masterfully bring to life. Each and every one of you breathes life into this book, and I honor you all.

To Daniela Rapp—without you and your belief in my vision, this book would not have come to life like it has. You help bring dreams into reality. Thank you.

To Robert (Bobby) Kennedy Jr., thank you brother, you are a beacon of love for so many and I honor you with of all my heart for the song that you are singing into remembrance for all.

To Tony Lyons, what can I say, without you, this book would not be. . . . Thank you for your trust and your compassion and for standing by my side in this journey.

I also wish to share a warm and heartfelt thanks to all of the Divine Mums and Dads in the MAHA movement that are choosing to show up for our children in ways that will evolve the system into its true nature, so that all may thrive and experience what true health feels like.

And of course, I must thank my lovely Mum, Joy, who shared with me her love of cooking and who always inspired me to follow my heart in life. I love you, Mum!

Cheers,
Pete xo
www.peteevans.com
Cook with love and laughter

Metric Conversions

If you're accustomed to using metric measurements, use these handy charts to convert the imperial measurements used in this book.

Weight (Dry Ingredients)

1 oz		30 g
4 oz	¼ lb	120 g
8 oz	½ lb	240 g
12 oz	¾ lb	360 g
16 oz	1 lb	480 g
32 oz	2 lb	960 g

Oven Temperatures

Fahrenheit	Celsius	Gas Mark
225°	110°	¼
250°	120°	½
275°	140°	1
300°	150°	2
325°	160°	3
350°	180°	4
375°	190°	5
400°	200°	6
425°	220°	7
450°	230°	8

Volume (Liquid Ingredients)

½ tsp.		2 ml
1 tsp.		5 ml
1 Tbsp.	½ fl oz	15 ml
2 Tbsp.	1 fl oz	30 ml
¼ cup	2 fl oz	60 ml
⅓ cup	3 fl oz	80 ml
½ cup	4 fl oz	120 ml
⅔ cup	5 fl oz	160 ml
¾ cup	6 fl oz	180 ml
1 cup	8 fl oz	240 ml
1 pt	16 fl oz	480 ml
1 qt	32 fl oz	960 ml

Length

¼ in	6 mm
½ in	13 mm
¾ in	19 mm
1 in	25 mm
6 in	15 cm
12 in	30 cm

Index

C

P

R

S

T

V

W

Y

Z